Lutheran Cooperation

through

Lutheran Higher Education

A Documentary History
of the
National Lutheran Educational Conference

1910 - 1967

By Gould Wickey

LUTHERAN EDUCATIONAL CONFERENCE OF
NORTH AMERICA
WASHINGTON, D.C.

1967

i

DEDICATED

To The Lutheran Educators
Who Caught The Vision of Larger Lutheran Unity
Through Cooperation in Lutheran Higher Education

Acknowledgements

The author wishes to thank the many persons who cooperated in supplying pictures of persons, places and events, and who helped supply some historical data not available in the records and proceedings of the National Lutheran Educational Conference on hand in the office.

TABLE OF CONTENTS

LIST OF PICTURES

The pictures of Groups are only those which were easily available. It is regretted that more pictures of the Martin Luther Fellows were not available. The pictures of individuals are of those persons, except for the officers of the first year, 1910, who held one or more offices for more than one year or were especially active and prominent on various committees helping to determine policies through the years. A few who served as presidents are noted in groups rather than in individual pictures, in the interest of economy. No special plan was used in listing the pictures, except those who were active in the early years are placed in the forepart.

PREFACE

The second decade of the twentieth century was significant in the history of the world and the history of the Lutheran Church in the United States and Canada. In that decade occurred the first world war with its devasting effects, and that same decade witnessed some very significant Lutheran Church mergers with constructive effects. In 1917 the Norwegian Lutheran Church of America (later called, The Evangelical Lutheran Church) was organized through the merger of the Synod for the Norwegian Lutheran Church in America (1853), Hauge's Norwegian Evangelical Lutheran Synod (1876), and United Norwegian Lutheran Church of America (1890). In 1918 was formed the United Lutheran Church in America through the union of The General Synod of the Evangelical Lutheran Church in the United States (1820), The United Synod of the Evangelical Lutheran Church in the South (1863), and The General Council of the Evangelical Luthern Church in North America (1867). Prior to these church mergers was the formation of the National Lutheran Editors' Association (1913), in which, it is reported, were representatives of all official Lutheran church periodicals and publications. Later, 1948, the NLEA amended its membership requirements by adding, "Editors of other Lutheran papers", provided there was the endorsement of editors of two official papers, but such members were not eligible to hold office in the organization. In 1914 was formed the Managers' Section of the National Lutheran Editors' Association.

Prior to all these Lutheran Church mergers and formation of national Lutheran organizations was the formation of the Lutheran Educational Conference in 1910 at Harrisburg, Pa. The word, National, was added to the name of the Conference at its sixth convention in 1919, making it read, National Lutheran Educational Conference. There is reason to believe that this Conference was influential in the formation of various Lutheran organizations and Lutheran Church Mergers. One basis for this statement is the fact that one of the founders of this Conference was Dr. F. G. Gotwald, who was secretary of the Board of Education of the General Synod and also editor of that Synod's paper, *Lutheran Church Work,* was one of the organizers of both the National Lutheran Editors' Association and the Managers' Section of that NLEA, and was active in the formation of the United Lutheran Church in America.

The story of the National Lutheran Educational Conference has never been written, but most of the facts are available. The Conference was never a promoter of itself; it lived to serve the colleges and seminaries and through them the Lutheran Church. The pictures of two Luther statues were purposely included at the beginning for they illustrate the two ultimate concurrent goals of this Conference throughout its history: the education and training of effective, evangelical preachers for the Lutheran Church, and the education and training of effective Christian teachers and citizens for the Church and the Country. It is quite fitting that this story of the Conference should be told.

At its meeting, on March 23, 1966 in Chicago, Illinois, the Executive Committee (Board of Directors) of the National Lutheran Educational Conference authorized its Executive Director, Gould Wickey, to prepare a *documentary* history of the Conference. As, such, no attempt has been made to prepare a *literary* history. The material for this story is taken from available minutes, printed programs, printed proceedings of annual meetings, and the files of the Conference. These sources speak for themselves with accuracy without embelishment and interpretation by the author. The history of any institution or organization is the story of people. For this reason a considerable number of pictures are included. These pictures of leaders and events tell more than thousands of words would convey. An attempt has been made to obtain pictures of those who have taken a prominent part in the development of the policies and programs of the Conference. Some of these persons are noted in group pictures rather than in individual pictures.

The action authorizing the preparation of this history was based primarily upon the fact that in January 1967, part of the program of services of this Conference was to be transferred to the Division of Educational Services of the Lutheran Council, United States of America (LCUSA), which Council was constituted at Cleveland, Ohio, November 16-18, 1966, and was scheduled to begin operation as of January 1, 1967. The Conference, as a corporate entity, will continue to hold annual meetings and fulfill certain objectives under the name, "Lutheran Educational Conference of North America."

The executive director of the Conference was chosen as the author of this history, no doubt because he had at hand in the office all the facts and documents on which to base such a documentary history, and also because he is no doubt the oldest living active member of the Conference, having joined in 1922, and during the period 1930-1967, has been an officer for fifteen years and the editor of the News Bulletin for twenty-three years.

This labor of love is performed with much joy since the author realizes that the facts connected with the Conference should be better known and should be made available to the libraries of Lutheran colleges, seminaries and universities, and certain university libraries where Lutherans are gathered and are doing research, as well as to Lutheran archives elsewhere.

That this history will be of value to the students of Lutheran higher education and of Lutheran church history in this generation and the future, is the cherished wish of the author.

Gould Wickey

March 1967
Washington, D.C.

LUTHER, THE PREACHER

A Statue on the Campus of Wartburg
Theological Seminary, Dubuque, Iowa

LUTHER, THE TEACHER
A Statue on the Campus of the Lutheran
Theological Seminary, Gettysburg, Pa.
Engraved on the side of the base are these words of Luther:
Truth is Mightier than Eloquence
The Spirit Stronger than Genius
Faith Greater than Learning.

CHAPTER I

Purpose, Organization and Administration

Purpose

The first paper presented at the first meeting of the Lutheran Educational Conference, held in Harrisburg, Penna., was entitled, "The Advantages of an Association of the Educational Forces of the Lutheran Church," by Professor A. J. Bowers of Newberry College. There is no record of the contents of that address, and nothing in the minutes would indicate a statement of purpose. Officers were elected and plans made for another meeting in 1911.

However, it seems from the various programs that there was "a cooperative interest and concern of all the educators of the Church" for the educational institutions of the Church. This is supported by a statement of Dr. F. G. Gotwald, who explained the object of the Conference. "The policy of this Conference", wrote Dr. Gotwald, "has not been exclusive but inclusive, and it has been the attempt of the Conference to include an interest in the work of higher education of all educational institutions of the Lutheran Church in America. There has been a gratifying response. A greater work than has yet been done remains to be done, and it is hoped that the various problems and the great task of the institutions of learning in the Lutheran Church in America may have the cooperative interest and concern of all the educators in the church, and that the National Lutheran Educational Conference will be the clearing house and one of the means used by all these educators to become better acquainted with each other and their tasks."

In a Handbook of Information, dated 1930 and authorized by the Executive Committee of the Conference, is found this concise sentence, "Its chief aim is to provide an agency through which the forces of Lutheran higher education in America may be mutually helpful."

The purpose as stated in the Constitution, approved January 6, 1958, is "to consider mutual problems in higher education, to share information, to suggest a strategy, and to encourage and to assist the member institutions in their programs of Lutheran higher education as they serve the Church and develop a Christian leadership for God and country."

1

Organization

The first meeting was held at Harrisburg, Penna., in Zion's Lutheran Church, on June 3, 1910. Present were representatives of the colleges and seminaries related to four Lutheran church bodies: the Joint Synod of Ohio, the General Synod, the General Council, and the United Synod of the South. It is worthwhile to record the names of those who attended that first meeting:

Rev. C. T. Aikens, President, Susquehanna University, Selinsgrove, Pa.

Rev. D. H. Bauslin, Professor, Hamma Divinity School, Springfield, Ohio

Rev. P. M. Bikle, Professor, Pennsylvania College, Gettysburg, Pa.

Rev. A. J. Bowers, Professor, Newberry College, Newberry, S. Carolina

George T. Ettinger, Professor, Muhlenberg College, Allentown, Pa.

Rev. R. L. Fritz, President, Lenoir College, Hickory, N. Carolina

Rev. J. L. van Gundy, Professor, Carthage College, Carthage, Illinois

Rev. F. G. Gotwald, Secretary, Board of Education, General Synod

Rev. J. A. W. Haas, President, Muhlenberg College, Allentown, Pa.

Rev. S. G. Hefelbower, President, Pennsylvania College, Gettysburg, Pa.

Rev. J. L. Kistler, Professor, Hartwick Seminary, N.Y.

Rev. Frank Manhart, Professor, Susquehanna University, Selinsgrove, Pa.

Rev. B. F. Prince, Professor, Wittenberg College, Springfield, Ohio

Franklin B. Sawvel, Professor, Thiel College, Greenville, Pa.

Rev. L. H. Schuh, President, Capital University, Columbus, Ohio

Rev. J. A. Singmaster, President, Lutheran Theological Seminary, Gettysburg, Pa.

E. M. Stahle, Principal, Glenville Academy, Glenville, Pa.

The officers elected for that meeting were: President, P. M. Bikle; Vice-President, L. H. Schuh; Second Vice-President, R. L. Fritz; and Secretary, F. B. Sawvel.

A list of all the officers for all the meetings held since 1910 is noted on the following pages.

The First Officers Elected in 1910

THE PRESIDENT
Philip M. Bikle, Ph.D.
Dean, Pennsylvania College
(now called, Gettysburg
College) Gettysburg, Pa.

THE SECRETARY
Franklin B. Sawvel, Ph.D.
*Professor and later President
Thiel College, 1914-1916*
Greenville, Pa.

3

The First Officers Elected in 1910

FIRST VICE-PRESIDENT
L. H. Schuh, Ph.D.
President, Capital University,
Columbus, Ohio

SECOND VICE-PRESIDENT
R. L. Fritz,
President, Lenoir College,
(now called Lenoir Rhyne
College)
Hickory, N.C.

4

A. J. Bowers,
Professor, Newberry College,
Newberry, S.C.
He read the first paper entitled,
"The Advantages of an Association of the Educational Forces of the L u t h e r a n Church."

C. T. Aikens,
President, Susquehanna University, Selinsgrove, Pa.

Benjamin F. Prince,
Professor, Wittenberg College,
Springfield, Ohio
Active at Wittenberg from
1866 to 1926. In latter years
was Vice-President.

J. A. Singmaster,
President, Lutheran Theological Seminary,
Gettysburg, Pa.

Frederick G. Gotwald
Secretary, Board of Education,
General Synod, and Editor,
Lutheran Church Work
NLEC
One of the organizers

John A. W. Haas, Ph.D.
President, Muhlenberg College,
Allentown, Pa.
NLEC
President, 1911

Harvey D. Hoover, Ph.D.
President, Carthage College
Carthage, Illinois
NLEC
Secretary, 1916-1921
President, 1922
Vice-President, 1923

John A. Morehead
President, Roanoke College
Salem, Virginia

CHRONOLOGICAL LIST OF OFFICERS

Date	President	Vice-President	Secretary	Treasurer	Executive Secretary
1910	P. M. Bikle	L. H. Schuh	F. B. Sawvell		
1911	J. A. Haas		F. P. Manhart		
1912	C. G. Heckert		C. T. Benze	Prof. Martzoff	
1913	No Record of a Meeting				
1914	No Record of a Meeting				
1915	No Record of a Meeting				
1916	J. Henry Harms	G. A. Andreen	H. D. Hoover	Otto Mees	
1917	No Meeting				
1918	G. A. Andreen		H. D. Hoover		
1919	W. A. Granville	L. A. Vigness	H. D. Hoover	J. Stump	
1920	L. A. Vigness	E. F. Pihlblad	H. D. Hoover	J. Stump	
1921	E. E. Stauffer	H. W. Elson	H. D. Hoover	J. Stump	
1922	H. D. Hoover		R. E. Tulloss	J. A. Aasgaard	
1923	Otto Mees	H. D. Hoover	R. E. Tulloss	H. J. Arnold	
1924	J. F. Krueger	J. A. Aasgaard	R. E. Tulloss	H. J. Arnold	
1925	L. W. Boe	O. J. Johnson	R. E. Tulloss	H. J. Arnold	

9

Year				
1926	G. A. Andreen	C. O. Solberg	R. E. Tulloss	H. J. Arnold
1927	R. E. Tulloss	E. F. Pihlblad	H. F. Martin	H. J. Arnold
1928	E. F. Pihlblad	J. N. Brown	H. F. Martin	H. J. Arnold
1929	J. N. Brown	W. P. Hieronymous	H. F. Martin	H. J. Arnold
1930	H. F. Martin	G. A. Andreen	Gould Wickey	H. J. Arnold
1931	O. J. Johnson	Otto Proehl	Gould Wickey	H. J. Arnold
1932	J. C. K. Preus	Wm. Young	Gould Wickey	H. J. Arnold
1933	Wm. Young	C. Bergendoff	Gould Wickey	H. J. Arnold
1934	Erland Nelson	J. Wargelin	Gould Wickey	H. J. Arnold
1935	H. W. A. Hanson	Arthur Wald	J. C. K. Preus	H. J. Arnold
1936	Conrad Bergendoff	Mary Markley	H. J. Arnold	H. J. Arnold
1937	Chas. J. Smith	C. M. Granskou	H. J. Arnold	H. J. Arnold
1938	C. M. Granskou	E. J. Braulick	H. J. Arnold	H. J. Arnold
1939	E. J. Braulick	J. C. Kinard	H. J. Arnold	H. J. Arnold
1940	J. C. Kinard	V. K. Nikander	H. J. Arnold	H. J. Arnold
1941	J. C. Kinard	V. K. Nikander	H. J. Arnold	H. J. Arnold
1942	H. J. Arnold	J. C. Kinard	F. C. Wiegman	F. C. Wiegman
1943	(Omitted: War-time Restrictions)			
1944	H. J. Arnold	J. C. Kinard	F. C. Wiegman	F. C. Wiegman
1945	B. M. Christensen	H. J. Arnold	F. C. Wiegman	F. C. Wiegman
1946	C. G. Shatzer	E. Lindquist	H. J. Arnold	H. J. Arnold

Year					
1947	E. Lindquist	W. P. Hieronymus	H. J. Arnold	H. J. Arnold	
1948	W. P. Hieronymus	T. F. Gullixon	H. J. Arnold	H. J. Arnold	
1949	J. N. Brown	H. L. Yochum	H. J. Arnold	H. J. Arnold	
1950	H. L. Yochum	L. M. Stavig	W. F. Zimmerman	W. F. Zimmerman	
1951	L. Tyson	E. M. Carlson	W. P. Hieronymus	W. P. Hieronymus	
1952	E. M. Carlson	R. E. Morton	Orville Dahl	Orville Dahl	
1953	R. E. Morton	C. H. Becker	Orville Dahl	Orville Dahl	
1954	C. H. Becker	V. R. Cromer	Orville Dahl	Orville Dahl	
1955	V. R. Cromer	O. P. Kretzmann	Orville Dahl	Orville Dahl	
1956	O. P. Kretzmann	C. C. Stoughton	Orville Dahl	Orville Dahl	
1957	C. C. Stoughton	E. B. Lawson	Orville Dahl	Orville Dahl	
1958	E. B. Lawson	J. W. Ylvisaker	Gould Wickey	Gould Wickey	Gould Wickey
1959	J. W. Ylvisaker	M. J. Neeb	Gould Wickey	Gould Wickey	Gould Wickey
1960	M. J. Neeb	L. M. Stavig	Gould Wickey	A. Barbara Wiegand	Gould Wickey
1961	L. M. Stavig	H. S. Oberly	Gould Wickey	A. Barbara Wiegand	Gould Wickey
1962	H. S. Overly	K. E. Mattson	Gould Wickey	A. Barbara Wiegand	Gould Wickey
1963	K. E. Mattson	A. O. Fuerbringer	Gould Wickey	A. Barbara Wiegand	Gould Wickey
1964	A. O. Fuerbringer	P. W. Dieckman	Gould Wickey	A. Barbara Wiegand	Gould Wickey
1965	P. W. Dieckman	R. L. Mortvedt	Gould Wickey	Chas. H. Solem	Gould Wickey
1966	R. L. Mortvedt	A. N. Rogness	Gould Wickey	Chas. H. Solem	Gould Wickey
1967	A. N. Rogness	Erling Jensen	Gould Wickey	Chas. H. Solem	Gould Wickey

11

Serious errors in the list of officers appeared in the printed proceedings beginning with the year 1931 and continued through to 1943. Those listed for 1931 should be deleted, and those listed for 1932 should be listed as for 1931, and each of the following years until and including 1940 should be listed for the year earlier. Then in 1940 should be recorded those as noted above. This records James C. Kinard as president for two years which is according to the minutes. Then there is confusion as to who was vice-president for the year 1942 The printed program does not agree with the minutes. It may be in this case that one elected as vice-president did not or could not function, and another was appointed.

An interpretation of this series of errors may be this: some one thought that the officers who preside and function at a meeting, say 1931, are those for that year. In reality the Conference has always elected in January the officers for that year and they did not function in a public meeting until the following year, unless a meeting was held during that year.

Another error was discovered in the printed proceedings from 1964 to 1967. The name of J. C. K. Preus is listed as executive director, when it should be listed as secretary, to which office he was elected in 1935. This is plainly the printer's error, which was not caught by proof-readers for four years.

Further, in the 1967 printed proceedings, the word, *Treasurer,* is placed in the line for the year 1960 when it should have been inserted a space immediately above, thereby having the name of Miss A. Barbara Wiegand begin appearing as treasurer for 1960 and continuing to and including 1964. Then, the name of Charles Solem should appear as treasurer beginning in 1965 and continuing in 1966 and 1967. Also in the 1967 proceedings, the name of Gould Wickey should appear as the executive director for 1966. In other words, the word, *Secretary,* should not appear in the line for the year 1966.

It is interesting to note the boards of education and the institutions from which the presidents were elected. In some cases it will be necessary to recognize an institution as having both a college and seminary. For example, Augustana College (Rock Island) and Seminary were not separated until 1948; Midland College operated Western Theological Seminary as a department from 1910 to 1949; Capital University had a college and a seminary until 1960; Wittenberg College operated both the college and Hamma Divinity School under one administration but Hamma was always considered a separate or graduate school and now the total institution has the name of Wittenberg University. Hence, it is difficult to say which school a president may have represented preeminently, unless it be the larger segment and that would generally be the college. In some cases, the seminary was started prior to the college, for example Augustana (Rock Island) and Capital. While it is not a serious matter, the author will need to use his judgment in denoting the institutions.

Boards of Education

Norwegian Lutheran Church: L. A. Vigness, 1920; J. C. K. Preus, 1932.

American Lutheran Church; William L. Young, 1933

Universities: Colleges and Seminaries

Augsburg: B. M. Christensen, 1945

Augustana (R.I.): G. A. Andreen, 1918, 1926; C. Bergendoff, 1936

Capital University: Otto Mees, 1923; H. L. Yochum, 1950

Wittenberg University: C. G. Heckert, 1912; R. E. Tulloss, 1927; Dean C. G. Shatzer, 1946; C. C. Stoughton, 1957

Seminaries

Augustana: K. E. Mattson, 1963

Concordia (St. Louis): A. O. Fuerbringer, 1964

Luther (St. Paul): A. N. Rogness, 1967

Colleges

Augustana, (S.D.): C. M. Granskou, 1938; L. M. Stavig, 1961

Bethany (Kan): E. F. Pihlblad, 1928; E. Lindquist, 1947

Carthage: H. D. Hoover, 1922

Concordia (Moorhead, Minn): J. N. Brown, 1929

Concordia Senior (Fort Wayne): M. J. Neeb, 1960

Dana: Erland Nelson, 1934; R. E. Morton, 1953

Gettysburg: Dean P. M. Bikle, 1910; W. A. Granville, 1919; H. W. A. Hanson, 1935

Gustavus Adolphus: O. J. Johnson, 1931; E. M. Carlson, 1952

Hartwick: H. J. Arnold, 1942, 1944

Lenoir Rhyne: V. R. Cromer, 1955

Luther (Ia): J. W. Ylivisaker, 1959

Midland: E. E. Stauffer, 1921; J. F. Krueger, 1924; H. F. Martin, 1930; W. P. Hieronymus, 1948; P. W. Dieckman, 1965

Muhlenberg: J. A. W. Haas, 1911; L. Tyson, 1951

Newberry: J. Henry Harms, 1916; J. C. Kinard, 1940, 1941

Pacific Lutheran University: Robert Mortvedt, 1966

Roanoke: C. J. Smith, 1937; H. S. Oberly, 1962

St. Olaf: L. W. Boe, 1925

Upsala: E. B. Lawson, 1958

Valparaiso University: O. P. Kretzmann, 1956

Wartburg: E. J. Braulick, 1940; C. H. Becker, 1954

It is quite evident that the larger and better established institutions did not dominate the elections. Likewise, with the boards of education, even though the United Lutheran Church was the largest church body which had a board represented in the Conference from the beginning, no president was elected from that Board. Dr. Mary E. Markley, a secretary of that Board, was elected vice-president in 1936 but was not advanced to the presidency the following year. Why? Perhaps the historian is supposed to narrate facts without asking the question why. However, in this case, this author heard the comment, "They objected to a women as president." I am inclined to think the real reason was: the secretary and treasurer at that time came from the ULCA, and the members wanted to distribute the offices among different institutions and church bodies. It is interesting to note that of the existing four year colleges, now members of the Conference, all but four had had representatives as president and all but two had some officer at some time, and these two became members only within the past five years. Considering that several institutions had both colleges and seminaries within their administrative organization, .the seminaries were well represented among the officers. A big factor in the representation was the interest which the school manifested in the meetings of the Conference. If an institution seldom had a representative at the meetings, it is natural that an officer would not be selected from that school. Institutions and boards of education were represented on the executive committee or board of directors and various factors would determine the selection of persons for the offices, such as distribution geographically and ecclesiastically, interest in attendance and participation, and availability. All institutions, except those recently received, have had membership in the Executive Committee or Board of Directors.

Membership

Memberships in the Conference have been of two kinds: institutional and individual. The institutional membership extends primarily to the administrative head thereof or his representative. Prior to 1926, faculty members as individuals became affiliated through the membership of the institution. In that year, however, the Conference took the following action:

> Resolved, that the provision by which teachers or administrative officers in institutions holding membership in the National Lutheran Educational Conference are by virtue of such membership, entitled to personal membership in the Conference is hereby rescinded.

Individual memberships have been open to Lutheran teachers or administrative officers in both Lutheran and non-Lutheran institutions of higher education, as well as to all pastors and church officials who are interested in the promotion and development of the Lutheran higher education in the United States and Canada.

While special mention is not made of the membership of boards of education of Lutheran church bodies or of the secretaries of such boards, it is quite evident that the secretaries of these boards did take a prominent part and exerted a desirable and constructive influence on the programs and work of the Conference. Mention has been made of the influence of Dr. F. G. Gotwald, secretary of the Board of Education of the former General Synod in the formation and organization of the Conference. Dr. L. A. Vigness, after he left the presidency of St. Olaf college, became the s e c r e t a r y of the Board of Education of the Norwegian Lutheran Church and appears as an active officer of this Conference. Dr. J. C. K. Preus, Dr. Orville Dahl, and Dr. Sidney Rand of the Board of Education of the Norwegian Lutheran Church, later called the Evangelical Lutheran Church, have been effective in the offices and committees of the Conference. Dr. William L. Young of the Board of Education of the American Lutheran Church was not only an active officer of the Conference but was much interested in special research projects. Dr. Robert Mortvedt, as executive of the Board of Education of the Augustana Lutheran Church, and later of the Board of Education of the Lutheran Church in America, took an active part in the affairs of the Conference and became its president in 1966 while president of the Pacific Lutheran University. Mr. Norman Fintel, executive of the Board of College Education of the American Lutheran Church, recently organized through merger in 1960, has manifested his interest in various ways. Dr. Arthur Ahlschwede, executive of the Board for Higher Education of The Lutheran Church-Missouri Synod, also takes his place with other such secretaries of Lutheran boards of education in his interest in the Conference. All secretaries of the Board of Education of the United Lutheran Church in America, formed in 1918 through merger, took an active part in the Conference, including, Dr. F. G. Gotwald, 1919-1925; Dr. C. S. Bauslin, 1918-1930, Dr. Mary E. Markley, 1919-1946; Dr. C. P. Harry, 1922-1946, Dr. Mildred E. Winston, 1928-1967, and Dr. Gould Wickey, 1929-1959. Each of these secretaries of this ULCA Board had particular responsibilities in said Board dealing with students, faculty and administration. This broadened the point of view of the Conference. With the formation of the Lutheran Church in America, two boards were authorized: the Board of College Education and Church Vocations, and the Board of Theological Education. The executives of these two boards, Dr. Francis C. Gamelin and Dr. E. Theodore Bachmann, have manifested their cooperation through support of the Conference's program of services and participation in the programs of the annual meetings.

Dues

In 1930 and for a period of time the scale of dues is listed as $25 for seminaries and colleges, $10 for junior colleges and academies, and $1 for individuals. At that time the Conference was holding annual meetings and printing the proceedings of the annual meetings and a directory of available Lutheran teachers. However, only three issues of the Directory of Teachers seemed to have been published and the proceedings of the annual meetings were not printed from 1943 to 1959 inclusive, apparently because the dues did not allow for such expenditures.

In 1958, when the Conference approved a plan to enlarge its program of services, the dues were radically changed. Church boards of education, collegiate and theological, were asked to contribute at least $500. Institutional dues were placed on a percentage basis of the General and Educational expenses of the previous academic year. In 1959 this percentage was finally fixed at 75/1000 percent for both colleges and seminaries. An associate membership of $25 was set up for those schools of less than 4-year status, which gave the schools "the right to attend meetings with voice but no vote, to receive proceedings and printed matter, to share in benefits of the Placement Bureau, but not the right to hold office and to share in the benefits of the Fellowship Program." Individual memberships were placed at $5.

As this history is being written in 1966, the membership includes 5 boards of higher education, college and theological, 14 seminaries, 31 colleges, 6 junior colleges, and 130 individuals. The Lutheran School of Theology in Chicago is counted as one functioning at three places: Maywood, and Rock Island, Illinois and Fremont, Nebraska in the fall of 1966 until the new buildings are ready at the new location near the University of Chicago.

Meetings, Places and Themes

Since 1910 the Conference held 52 meetings, the exceptions being 1913, 1914, 1915, 1917, and 1943. It is known that in 1943 there were definite wartime restrictions; in 1917 the same may have been true. For 1913, 1914, and 1915 no records are available and it appears as though no meetings were held, although the meeting of 1912 provided for a committee to prepare a program for a 1913 meeting, but the meeting of 1918 was called the fifth meeting, which confirms the judgment that no meetings were held 1913, 1914, 1915, and 1917. There is no question about the omission of the meeting in 1943.

A summary of the places of meeting and the number of times at each place shows Chicago 9, Atlantic City 5, Cincinnati 5, New York 5, Washington 4, Philadelphia 3, St. Louis 2, Boston 2, Cleveland 2, Los Angeles 2, and once at each of the following: Atlanta, Ga., Baltimore, Md., Chattanooga, Tenn., Denver, Col., Gettysburg, Pa., Harrisburg, Pa., Indianapolis, Ind., Kansas City, Mo., Louisville, Ky., Marion, Va., Maywood, Ill., Miami, Fla., and Springfield, O.

An exhibit of the annual meetings follows, showing the year, the place, and the general theme. It appears that 1933 was the first year that a general theme was indicated.

DATES, PLACES, AND THEMES OF ANNUAL MEETINGS

Date	Place	Theme
June 1910	Harrisburg, Pa.	
April 1911	Gettysburg, Pa.	
Dec. 1912	Springfield, O	
1913	No meeting held	
1914	No meeting held	
1915	No meeting held	
Jan. 1916	Maywood, Ill.	
1917	No meeting, probably on account of war conditions	
Jan. 1918	Chicago, Ill.	
Jan. 1919	Chicago, Ill.	
Jan. 1920	Chicago, Ill.	
Jan. 1921	New York, N.Y.	
Jan. 1922	Chicago, Ill.	
Jan. 1923	Chicago, Ill.	
Jan. 1924	New York, N.Y.	
Jan. 1925	Chicago, Ill.	
Jan. 1926	New York, N.Y.	
Jan. 1927	Chicago, Ill.	
Jan. 1928	Atlantic City, N.J.	
Jan. 1929	Chattanooga, Tenn.	
Mar. 1930	Chicago, Ill.	
Jan. 1931	Indianapolis, Ind.	
Jan. 1932	Cincinnati, Ohio	
Jan. 1933	Atlantic City, N.J.	Cooperation in Lutheran Higher Education
Jan. 1934	St. Louis, Mo.	Lutheran Higher Education in a Changing World Order
Jan. 1935	Atlanta, Ga.	Making Spiritual Values Supreme in Lutheran Higher Education
Jan. 1936	New York, N.Y.	Development of Christian Personality —the Major Objective in Christian Higher Education
Jan. 1937	Washington, D.C.	The Christian College and American Citizenship
Jan. 1938	Chicago, Ill.	Greater Faith, Greater Hope, Greater Service for Christian Education

Jan. 1939	Louisville, Ky.	The Christian College—Bulwark of Democracy
Jan. 1940	Philadelphia, Pa.	Vital Fronts in Christian Higher Education
June 1941	Marion, Va.	An Examination of Present Practices in Lutheran Colleges
Jan. 1942	Baltimore, Md.	Building the Kind of World We Want to Live In
1943	Meeting omitted on account of War Restrictions	
Jan. 1944	Cincinnati, O.	Our Lutheran Colleges in War and After
Jan. 1945	Atlantic City, N.J.	The College-Supported Church
Jan. 1946	Cleveland, O.	Christian Higher Education and Lutheran World Unity
Jan. 1947	Boston, Mass.	The Place of Christian Higher Education in Lutheran World Action
Jan. 1948	Cincinnati, O.	Design for Lutheran Higher Education Today
Jan. 1949	New York, N.Y.	Design for Lutheran Higher Education Tomorrow
Jan. 1950	Cincinnati, O.	Our Task
Jan. 1951	Atlantic City, N.J.	Days of Destiny for Christian Higher Education
Jan. 1952	Washington, D.C.	Christian Higher Education and the Conscience of Our Time
Jan. 1953	Los Angeles, Cal.	New Horizons in Lutheran Higher Education
Jan. 1954	Cincinnati, O.	Current Issues in Lutheran Higher Education
Jan. 1955	Washington, D.C.	The Theological Foundation for Lutheran Higher Education
Jan. 1956	St. Louis, Mo.	Current Topic for Colleges and Seminaries
Jan. 1957	Philadelphia, Pa.	Our Lutheran Higher Education, 1956-1970
Jan. 1958	Miami, Fla.	The National Lutheran Educational Conference: A Reexamination of its Task for the Future
Jan. 1959	Kansas City, Mo.	The Christian Teacher—Channel of Excellence
Jan. 1960	Boston, Mass.	New Dimensions in Lutheran Higher Education

Jan. 1961	Denver, Colo.	The Liberal Arts and Lutheran Higher Education
Jan. 1962	Cleveland, O.	Current Influences Related to Lutheran Higher Education
Jan. 1963	Atlantic City, N.J.	Factors in the Long Look for Lutheran Higher Education
Jan. 1964	Washington, D.C.	Creative Tensions
Jan. 1965	St. Louis, Mo.	Educational Integrity and Church Responsibility
Jan. 1966	Philadelphia, Pa.	Campus Rebellions and Constructive Changes
Jan. 1967	Los Angeles, Cal.	Academic Involvement in the Ongoing Reformation

Re-organization and Incorporation

At the 1957 annual meeting there was a definite concensus that the work of the Conference must be re-examined and that steps be taken, if possible, to effect a larger program of service. Accordingly, it was resolved,

"That the executive committee be authorized and directed to study the plans for the f u t u r e re-organization of the NLEC in light of potential changes in the Secretaryship, and that the Committee report at the next meeting of the NLEC."

The Conference had been informed by Dr. Orville Dahl, that he had resigned his position with the Division of Higher Education of the Evangelical Lutheran Church, and that during the period, 1952-1957, when he was privileged to hold the office of secretary-treasurer, "the bulk of the work was made possible by the office staff of the Division of Higher Education, ELC, which had contributed its time as well as supplies." Dr. Dahl further declared, "that the work of the NLEC was not being advanced by an officer working on a voluntary, part-time basis without a budget or a program." The Conference had also been informed that Gould Wickey would retire in 1959 from his position of executive secretary of the Board of Education of the United Lutheran Church in America.

At that same meeting in 1957, the Conference asked the Executive Committee to prepare a plan which will enable the program of the Conference to be carried on. It also appointed a special committee on fellowships for teachers, hoping that some plan could be devised whereby a sum of money would be available for the training of teachers who would become members of the faculties of the Lutheran colleges and seminaries.

19

As a member of the Executive Committee of the Conference for 1958 and having been an officer for many years interested in the expansion of the program of the Conference, Gould Wickey prepared a suggested plan for the larger program of the Conference. This was presented to the presidents of the colleges of the ULCA, to the Board of Higher Education, ULCA, and to other Lutheran college presidents as occasion permitted. A revised statement was submitted to some 26 presidents and deans of Lutheran colleges and seminaries gathered in Minneapolis during August 1957 for the meeting of the Lutheran World Federation, after having been approved in principle by the Executive Committee of the Conference. While in Rock Island, the plan was discussed with Dr. Conrad Bergendoff, president of Augustana College, who was chairman of the special committee on Faculty Fellowships. The whole plan appealed to him and he indicated that the plan accomplished what his committee would need to do so far as faculty fellowships were concerned. With some changes suggested at the Minneapolis meeting of the Executive Committee, the Plan was submitted to the 1958 annual meeting of the Conference in Miami, Fla., for official action.

This report of Dr. Wickey, after giving a historical sketch of the Conference and an evaluation of the program of the Conference at that time, presented a suggested expanded program which included, without stating the details here, (1) a Teachers (Placement) Bureau with a full-time secretary, (2) a program of Graduate Fellowships for persons now teaching or agreeing to teach or serve in a Lutheran college or seminary, (3) a News Bulletin, to be issued five times a year and to be sent in bulk to all faculty members of all institutional members of the Conference and individually to the members of the boards of directors of Lutheran colleges and seminaries, directors of Boards of Education of Lutheran Church bodies, to church officials and to individual members of the Conference, (4) Research and Studies to be under the direction of the Executive Committee or a special Committee, (5) Annual Meetings with general sessions and if possible sectional meetings for seminaries, colleges, junior colleges, and training schools, and (6) other possible services, such as liaison with government and national educational agencies, counseling with institutions as time permits, conferences, regional or national, of faculty groups, contacts at the annual meetings of professional associations seeking persons interested in teaching at Lutheran colleges and seminaries, and microfilming for Lutheran schools after the purchase of necessary equipment and as requested.

This report further indicated the necessary facilities, equipment and personnel necessary to carry such a program at the beginning. It also suggested a budget for 1958 and a suggested plan of dues from the schools on a percentage basis.

The concluding statement of the report declared such a program (1) is needed and relevant to the problems of our Lutheran schools, (2) is bold and imaginative, (3) has possibilities of significant service to Lutheran colleges and seminaries, (4) is realistic, (5) is conservative, and (6) is challenging.

After due discussion in an atmosphere of optimism, the Conference unanimously voted to re-organize on the basis of the suggested plan, to establish an office in Washington, D.C., to accept the offer of some furniture and equipment, necessary for the office, from the Board of Education, ULCA., which moved to New York in January 1958, to elect Gould Wickey as Executive Director on a part-time basis at a salary of $2,500 beginning February 1, 1958, to incorporate in the District of Columbia, to qualify, the newly incorporated NLEC with the Internal Revenue Office, to solicit donations for the Fellowship Program, to accept a system of dues on a percentage basis of the general and educational expense of the school, and to make any necessary changes in the Constitution.

The office was set up in the Lutheran Church Center at 2633—16th Street, N.W., Washington, D.C. as of February 1, 1958, and Gould Wickey began his service as a part-time executive director on the same date.

Copies of the Certificate of Incorporation and the Constitution follow on succeeding pages.

CERTIFICATE OF INCORPORATION

We, the undersigned, all citizens of the United States and a majority residents of the District of Columbia, of full age, desiring to associate ourselves as a corporation pursuant to the provisions of Title 29 of Chapter 6 of the District of Columbia Code (1951), do hereby certify as follows:

FIRST: The name and title by which this corporation shall be known in law shall be

NATIONAL LUTHERAN EDUCATIONAL CONFERENCE.

SECOND: The term for which it is organized shall be perpetual.

THIRD: The particular business and objects of said corporation shall be:

To consider mutual problems in higher education, to share information, to suggest a common strategy, and to encourage the member institutions in their program of Lutheran higher education as they serve the Church and develop a Christian leadership for God and country. The attainment of these objects shall include the receipt, holding and dispensing of funds and property.

FOURTH: The number of its trustees, directors or managers for the first year of existence shall be ten (10).

IN TESTIMONY WHEREOF we have this 28th day of February 1958, hereunto set our hands and seals.

/s/ Clarence T. Nelson (SEAL)

/s/ J. Victor Murtland (SEAL)

/s/ Gould Wickey (SEAL)

This Certificate was signed and sealed before, and notarized by Marian G. Shocket, Notary Public in and for the District of Columbia on 28 February 1958.

CONSTITUTION
of the
NATIONAL LUTHERAN EDUCATIONAL CONFERENCE
As Approved Jan. 6, 1958

Article I. Name

The name of this association shall be

NATIONAL LUTHERAN EDUCATIONAL CONFERENCE

Article II. Purpose

The purpose of this Conference shall be to consider mutual problems in higher education, to share information, to suggest a strategy, and to encourage and to assist the member institutions in their programs of Lutheran higher education as they serve the Church and develop a Christian leadership for God and country.

The attainment of this purpose shall include the receipt, holding and dispensing of funds and property.

Article III. Membership

1. The National Lutheran Educational Conference shall be an association of institutions of higher education of the Lutheran bodies in the United States and Canada. Each institution may be represented by its president and by such other persons as he shall designate, but for formal voting each institution shall have but one vote.

2. The membership shall include also Boards of Education of the Lutheran bodies, individuals interested in its purpose as may care to join, and other Lutheran educational agencies or groups as the Conference

may from time to time elect into membership.

Article IV. Officers

1. Officers shall be: a president, a vice-president, and a secretary-treasurer. The duties of each officer shall be the usual ones for the office.

2. Other officers may be elected from time to tome.

3. The terms of office shall be determined by the Conference.

Article V. Executive Committees and Its Powers

1. *Composition.* There shall be an Executive Committee composed of the officers, the immediate past president, the Chairman of the Commission on Records and Research, and five members at large to be elected annually by the members present at the meeting. One member of the Executive Committee shall always be a seminary representative.

2. *Powers.* The Executive Committee shall have power to determine who shall be authorized on the Corporation's behalf to sign bills, notes, receipts, acceptances, endorsements, checks, releases, contracts and documents.

The Executive Committee shall be responsible for the program of each annual meeting and shall be empowered to carry on necessary business between the annual meetings. It shall meet as often as necessary.

Article VI. Commissions and Standing Committees

There shall be a Commission on Records and Research, comprising the chief executive of each member Board of Higher Education. This commission shall have responsibility for any items or projects of research which may be referred to it by the Conference.

There may be such other commissions or standing committees as the Conference may decide from time to time.

Article VII. Dues, Gifts and Grants

The annual dues of institutional and individual members of the Conference shall be determined by the Conference from time to time.

Gifts may be received from individuals and grants from foundations or charitable agencies to be used for the purposes and program of the Conference.

Article VIII. Meetings

Meetings shall be held annually, and, generally, in conjunction with the meetings of the Association of American Colleges.

Special meetings may be called by the Executive Committee at such time and place as may be decided.

Article IX. Amendments

This Constitution may be amended at any meeting of the Conference, provided the proposed amendment has been presented at a session and is voted on at a later session.

SIGNING THE ARTICLES OF INCORPORATION, 1958

In the office of the NLEC
Standing, (left), Rev. J. Victor Murtland, Pastor, Grace Lutheran Church, Washington, D.C., and Rev. Clarence T. Nelson, Pastor, Augustana Lutheran Church Washington, D.C. Seated, Gould Wickey.

Gould Wickey, Ph.D.

Executive Secretary, Board of Education, ULCA, 1929-1959

NLEC

Member, 1922—
Editor, News Bulletin,
1932-1934, 1948-1966
Secretary, 1930-1934, 1967
Secretary-Treasurer, 1958-59
Secretary and Executive Director,
1958-1966

24

O. P. Kretzmann, Ph.D.

President, Valparaiso University

NLEC
Vice-President, 1955
President, 1956

Conrad Bergendoff, Ph.D.

President, Augustana College
(Ill.)

NLEC
Vice-President, 1933
President, 1936

C. M. Granskou

President, Augustana College,

NLEC
Vice-President, 1937
President, 1938

C. C. Stoughton

President, Wittenberg College

NLEC
Vice-President, 1956
President, 1957

TREASURERS OF THE CONFERENCE

A. Barbara Wiegand

NLEC
Treasurer, 1960-1964

Chas. H. Solem

Graduate, St. Olaf College
NLEC
Treasurer, 1965

27

Through the Years from 1910 to 1958 the Office of the NLEC existed wherever the Secretary had an office. In 1958 the office was officially established in the Lutheran Church Center (4th floor left), 2623 – 16th Street, N.W., Washington, D.C.

The Board of Directors during 1966. Reading from left to right are (standing): Dr. A. G. Huegli, vice-president, Valparaiso University; Dr. Paul Dieckman, president, Midland College and President, NLEC, 1965; Dr. Erling Jensen, president, Muhlenberg College; Dr. Edgar Carlson, president, Gustavus Adolphus College and president, NLEC, 1952; (seated) Dr. Gould Wickey, executive director, NLEC; Dr. Robert Mortvedt, president, Pacific Lutheran University, and president, NLEC, 1966; and Dr. Alvin Rogness, president, Luther Seminary, and president, NLEC, 1967. Not present: Dr. John Bachman, president, Wartburg College, and Charles Solem, Treasurer, NLEC, 1965-.

A Revised Constitution

The Constitution as adopted in 1958 served the Conference well, except that it was not explicit as to the powers of the Executive Committee or Board of Directors, it did not have any statement as to the authority of the Conference, it combined what is generally in bylaws with the constitution, and it had no direction as to special meetings. There may have been some other minor omissions. In light of these facts and the further condition that there would be established a Lutheran Council in the United States and one in Canada, each with a division of educational services, with the consequence that there would be no agency to serve all Lutheran schools and educators in both countries whether or not related to the Lutheran church bodies which formed the mentioned Lutheran Councils, it was deemed desirable and necessary to have a revised constitution prepared. This the executive director was authorized to do. Such constitution and bylaws were prepared by the executive and presented to the Executive Committee at meetings held in Los Angeles January 15 and 16, 1967. They were approved and presented to the business session of the Annual Meeting January 16, 1967. On account of the time schedule, the document was not considered in detail but was accepted in principle and the Board of Directors was authorized to proceed under the Constitution and Bylaws as presented. It is deemed desirable that this document be included in this history, and accordingly it follows.

THE CONSTITUTION AND BYLAWS
of the
LUTHERAN EDUCATIONAL CONFERENCE
OF NORTH AMERICA
PREAMBLE

Whereas, the National Lutheran Educational Conference was organized in 1910 in order to provide a free association whereby the representatives of Lutheran colleges and seminaries and other Lutheran educators could gather together from time to time and could discuss problems related to Lutheran higher education, could keep members mutually informed of developments at the various institutions, both Lutheran and non-Lutheran, and could make suggestions whereby Lutheran higher education could become more effective in its service to church and country; and

Whereas, the distinctive program of services of the National Lutheran Educational Conference is being transferred to the Division of Educational Services of the *Lutheran Council, United States of America,* as of January 31, 1967; and

Whereas, there is continued need for a free association of Lutheran higher education to fulfill such functions as were expressed in 1910 and to include Lutheran educational institutions and Lutheran educators beyond those now included in any existing Lutheran agency or organization; and

Whereas, the National Lutheran Educational Conference at its annual meeting in Philadelphia, Pennsylvania, January 8-10, 1966, voted unanimously to continue the National Lutheran Educational Conference as a corporate entity;

Therefore, representatives of Lutheran colleges, seminaries, universities, and boards of higher education do hereby agree to continue a free association of Lutheran educators, related to both Lutheran and non-Lutheran educational institutions in Canada and the United States, interested in Lutheran higher education, and to be governed by the following Constitution and Bylaws.

THE CONSTITUTION

Article I.   Name and Incorporation

Section 1.   Name

The name of this association shall be

LUTHERAN EDUCATIONAL CONFERENCE
OF NORTH AMERICA

hereinafter r e f e r r e d to as "Conference," (formerly called, National Lutheran Educational Conference).

Section 2.   Incorporation

This Conference shall be incorporated.

Article II.   Purpose

The purpose of this Conference shall be to consider problems in higher education, especially as related to Lutheran higher education, to share information, to suggest strategy, and to encourage and to assist the member institutions in their programs of Lutheran higher education as they serve the Lutheran Church and develop a Christian leadership for Church and Country.

The attainment of this purpose shall include the receipt, holding and dispensing of funds and property.

Article III.   Functions

The functions of this Conference shall be:

1. to provide a free forum in which the representatives of Lutheran institutions of higher education and of various Lutheran boards, organizations, agencies, and Lutheran individuals related or not related to Lutheran schools may discuss their mutual problems and

their concerns about higher education, especially Lutheran higher education, collegiate and theological.

2. to cooperate with the Divisions of Educational Services of the Lutheran Council in the U.S.A. and Lutheran Council in Canada in service to Lutheran higher education.

Article IV. Authority

The recommendations of this Conference regarding Lutheran higher education shall be wholly advisory and suggestive to Lutheran educational institutions. Whenever authorized, a designated officer may present the Conference's judgment on pertinent questions to Lutheran and non-Lutheran agencies and groups. The Conference shall present a report of its activities to its membership.

Article V. Membership

Membership shall be open to all Lutheran educational institutions, boards, organizations, agencies, and to individuals interested in Lutheran higher education, in Canada and the United States. Accordingly, there shall be three classes of membership:

1. *Institutions:* Colleges, Seminaries and Universities;
2. *Organizations:* Boards, Organizations and Agencies; and
3. *Individuals* in Lutheran and non-Lutheran educational institutions, and others interested in Lutheran higher education.

The dues for each class of membership shall be determined by the Conference from time to time on recommendation of the Board of Directors

Article VI. Meetings

Section 1. There shall be an annual meeting of the Conference.

Section 2. Special meetings may be called by the Board of Directors.

Section 3. One-third of the representatives of member institutions and organizations in attendance shall constitute a quorum.

Section 4. Each official representative of member institutions and organizations shall be notified at least fifteen days prior to the date of the meeting.

Article VII. Officers

Section 1. The officers shall include a president, a vice-president, a secretary and a treasurer, to be elected at the annual convention for a term of one year. The vice-president shall be the president-elect. The offices of secretary and treasurer may be held by one person if the conference so decides at any regular meeting.

Section 2. All officers shall take office at the conclusion of the meeting at which they are elected and shall continue to serve in such capacity until their successors assume office.

Section 3. The officers of the Conference shall serve in the same capacities as officers of the Board of Directors.

Section 4. The Conference shall select such other officers or staff as conditions may require.

Article VIII. Board of Directors, Committees and Commissions

Section 1. Board of Directors

a. *Composition.* There shall be a Board of Directors, which shall serve as a board of trustees of the Corporation, composed of the officers and five members at large. The membership of this Board of Directors shall be representative of the various geographical areas as well as the different educational institutions, organizations, and agencies which may be members of the Conference. At least one member of the Board of Directors shall always be a seminary representative.

b. *Powers.* The Board of Directors shall have the power to determine who shall be authorized on behalf of the Conference (Corporation) to sign bills, notes, receipts, acceptances, endorsements, checks, releases, contracts, and documents.

The Board of Directors shall have the power to carry on any necessary business between annual meetings, and shall be vested with all the powers of the Conference which are not otherwise reserved or delegated.

The Board of Directors shall meet as often as may be necessary to carry on the business of the Conference, making a report of such meetings at the time of the annual meeting.

The Board of Directors shall have such other powers and functions as may be listed in the Bylaws and assigned by the Conference from time to time.

Section 2. Committees may be appointed, from time to time, especially in connection with annual or special meetings.

Section 3. Commissions may be appointed to make special and extended studies or to perform functions for special conditions and situations.

Article IX. Financial Matters

Section 1. The regular financial support of the Conference shall be derived mainly from the dues received from the member institutions, boards, organizations, agencies, and individuals. These dues shall be determined by the Conference from time to time.

Section 2. The conference may receive grants and gifts from foundations and other sources for projects and services.

Section 3. No funds shall be borrowed on behalf of the Conference except any temporary loan as may be necessary to carry on the work of the Conference, and then only with the unanimous approval of the Board of Directors.

Article X. Bylaws

Bylaws consistent and in harmony with the Constitution of this Conference may be adopted or amended by a two-thirds vote of the representatives and members present and qualified to vote, at a regularly called meeting of the Conference, provided that notice of each proposed amendment shall have been presented at a session and voted on at a subsequent session of the same meeting. A provision of the Bylaws may be suspended by a three-fourths vote of the representatives and members present and voting at any meeting.

Article XI. Amendments

Amendments of this Constitution may be proposed in writing at any meeting of the Conference or of the Board of Directors. Notice of such proposed amendment shall be mailed by the secretary to all the duly appointed representatives of member institutions and organizations at least thirty days before the date of the meeting at which the proposed amendment shall be considered. A two-thirds vote of the representatives present and voting at such meeting shall be required for the adoption of an amendment.

BYLAWS

Section I. The Place of Business

The place of business shall be Washington, D.C.

Section II. Meetings

Item 1. The regular meeting shall be held at such time and place as the Board of Directors may decide or the Conference may authorize.

Item 2. Special meetings of the Conference may be called for specified purposes by action of the Board of Directors, and shall be called by the secretary of the Conference upon the written request of at least 20 of the duly appointed representatives and members who attended the previous meeting of the Conference. The Board of Directors shall determine the time and place of a special meeting. The notice for a special meeting shall be mailed to the duly appointed representatives of institutions and boards, at least fifteen days in advance of the date of said special meeting and such notice shall state explicitly the business to be considered at the meeting.

Item 3. Robert's Rules of Order, latest edition, shall be the governing parliamentary law of the Conference except as may be otherwise provided in the constitution or bylaws.

Section III. Representation and Membership

Item 1. The representatives of Lutheran educational institutions, organizations, and agencies, which have decided to participate in this Conference, shall be selected in such manner as each institution and organization may determine. Each member institution and organization may have

34

not more than two representatives with voting power. The term of office of such representatives shall be determined by each educational institution or organization.

Item. 2. Persons who are members of the Conference but not representatives of educational institutions or organizations shall have the right of participation in discussions. Their terms of membership shall be a full calendar year of 12 months so that each may receive copies of printed proceedings of annual meetings.

Section IV. Elections

Item 1. In the election of the officers: president, vice-president, secretary and treasurer, a majority of the votes cast shall elect.

Item 2. In case a vacancy occurs in said offices, the Board of Directors may make an ad interim appointment, if such be necessary, before the next annual meeting.

Section V. Officers

Item 1. The president shall preside at all meetings of the Conference and of the Board of Directors, appoint any committees not otherwise provided for, and see that the Constitution and Bylaws are observed and the enactments of the Conference are carried out. He shall execute any contracts authorized by the Conference and requiring his signature and such other instruments as may be authorized by the Conference or by the Board of Directors. He shall have voice in all meetings of any standing committee and of all other committees of the Conference, or he may appoint another officer to represent him in the meetings of said committees.

Item 2. The vice-president shall perform all the duties of the president in his absence or incapacity.

Item 3. The secretary shall record the minutes of the meetings of the Conference and of the Board of Directors. The minutes of the Conference shall be transmitted to each representative of the member institutions and organizations. He shall transmit notices of all meetings to the representatives of the member institutions and organizations, and notices of all meetings of the Board of Directors to the members thereof.

Item 4. The treasurer shall receive and disburse all monies on proper vouchers and authorizations, keeping an accurate record of all financial transactions and reporting thereon to the annual meeting of the Conference, and sending statements to the Board of Directors as may be requested.

Section VI. The Board of Directors

Item 1. The Board of Directors shall meet as such times and places as may be necessary to conduct its business.

Item 2. A majority of the members of the Board of Directors shall constitute a quorum.

Item 3. The Board of Directors shall have the following duties and functions, in addition to the powers granted in the Constitution:

    a.   to exercise trusteeship responsibilities for the Conference.

    b.   to provide an agenda and a program for each regular and special meeting of the Conference.

    c.   to recommend annual budgets for adoption at the annual meeting of the Conference

    d.   to be the Nominating Committee, presenting a list of officers and the additional members of the Board of Directors for the ensuing year. Other nominations are allowed from the floor.

    e.   To plan for any publications, which the Conference may authorize.

Section VII.   Committees and Commissions

Item. 1.   The *Officers of the Board of Directors* shall be the *Executive Committee,* performing such functions as may be requested from time to time.

Item 2.   *Committee on Resolutions.* The president shall appoint a committee on resolutions for each annual meeting.

Item 3.   *Other Committees/Commissions* may be appointed as may be necessary

Section VIII.   Staff

If the functions of this Conference require an unusual and extended amount of service by any officer, or other appointed person, with required secretarial or other assistance, the Board of Directors shall make payment for such services, as may be mutually agreed.

Section IX.   Financial Meetings

Item 1.   The *fiscal year* shall be the calendar year.

Item 2.   There shall be an *annual audit* of the financial records and accounts.

Item 3.   The Conference shall provide a *BLANKET FIDELITY BOND* in an amount to be specified by the Board of Directors to cover the officers and any and all employees who handle funds on behalf of the Conference, the premium thereon being paid by the Conference.

Item 4.   Officers shall not be compensated for their usual services.

Item 5.   The expenses of members of the Board of Directors, of special committees, and of commissions in performance of their responsibilities shall be paid on the basis of expense vouchers provided by the Conference and approved by the secretary before payment.

Item 6.   *Dues.*   The dues for membership shall be adequate to cover the general costs for operating the Conference.   The annual dues shall be determined by the Conference.

> —Approved in principal by the annual meeting of
> the National Lutheran Educational Conference
> January 16, 1967

Special Arrangements for 1967

At the annual meeting of the Conference, held January 15-16, 1967 in Los Angeles, the Conference elected Gould Wickey secretary for the period 1967-1968, under a constitutional provision which requires the election of officers annually. This has been the policy of the Conference throughout its history. In the interest of financial economy and the economy of time of the secretary, the records and files were moved to the home of the secretary where the office was established within the Washington postal area. The responsibility assigned to the secretary for the year 1967 was preparing the manuscripts for printing in the proceedings of the annual meeting and attending to the mailing thereof, completing the documentary history of the Conference and attending to its printing and distribution and screening of all files and records, and organizing the material for the archives of the Conference. His responsibility also includes planning for the meetings of the Board of Directors and planning for the program and detailed arrangements of the annual meeting. For the unusual services of the secretary during 1967 some salary and allowances were allowed.

The furniture, most of the equipment, all the files pertaining to the Placement Service, and all information and facilities regarding the News Bulletin were transfered to the Washington Office of the Division of Educational Service, Lutheran Council in the United States of America on January 31, 1967, with Mr. Howard Holcomb serving as Assistant Executie Secretary of the Division and in charge of the Washington Office.

The secretary of the Lutheran Educational Conference of North America rendered such services to Mr. Holcomb as was necessary to assist him in taking over certain services and becoming acquainted with certain educational offices in Washington.

Finances

Finances are generally a problem in most church and educational organizations. In the early years of the Conference not many comments were made about finances. In 1919 the Conference started to print the proceedings and sometimes the secretary had to express regret that the printer's bill was not paid. Printing of three issues of the Directory of Lutheran Teachers required special assessments. From 1942 to 1959 no proceedings were printed because of lack of funds, although some persons thought some of the proceedings were not worth printing.

When the secretaries were presidents or professors of colleges, and secretaries of church boards of education, the expenses included the printing of programs, the cost of mailing the news bulletin from 1933 to 1957, and the printing of the proceedings, when they were printed. The offices of the secretaries gave much time and utilized the facilities and supplies of those offices which would have amounted to considerable sums. In the early years, 1919 and following for a few years, the records indicated that the printed proceedings were sold, thereby keeping the Conference out of debt. The expenses in 1919 amounted to $31.91.

At the 1921 meeting, Secretary H. D. Hoover, in giving a financial report, frankly said, "The Secretary had to take some risks (financial) in pushing the work of the Conference and assume some responsibility which might seem as though he was assuming undue authority. We hope that this Conference will accept the Secretary's explanation that all was done in sincere humility for the welfare of the cause."

In 1922, from each school desiring membership in the Conference, the secretary was authorized to collect the sum of five dollars ($5.00). But in 1930, as noted in the section under Membership, the dues became for seminaries and colleges $25.00, for junior colleges and academies $10.00, and for individuals $1. In spite of this increase in income the proceedings could not be printed from 1942 to 1959.

In 1958, for eleven months, the expenditures amounted to $13,854.80. For the full year of 1959, the treasurer reports an income of $45,125.17 and expenditures of $30,569.70, with $14,555.47 on hand, but of this balance $10,124 would be paid out in January of 1960 for faculty fellowships. In that year the Lilly Foundation contributed $20,000 of a promised $50,000 towards the Faculty Fellowship Program.

In 1965, the last full year for the Faculty Fellowship program, the expenditures amounted to $44,794.93, of which $19,200 was for fellowships. In that year the salary and allowances for the executive director were $6,500, and for the office staff $7,283.50.

The Conference closed out its extended program in January 1967 with a sizeable balance which covered the whole budget for 1967.

Some may inquire about the distribution of the institutional dues as pertains to the institutions related to the three church bodies. The following exhibit for the institutional dues paid in 1964 will answer that question, and is representative of the various years during the period 1958-1966:

Institutional Dues Paid in 1964
(The numbers in brackets indicate the number of schools)

	Colleges	Seminaries	Total	Percent
American Lutheran Church	$10,524.08	$ 693.14	$11,217.22	35.56%
	[12]	[4]	[16]	
Lutheran Church in America	15,155.48	1,371.61	16,527.09	52.40%
	[21]	[11]	[32]	
Lutheran Church-Mo. Synod	2,713.79	1,082.22	3,796.01	12.04%
	[3]	([2]	[5]	
Total	28,393.35	3,146.97	$31,540.32	100.00%

It is interesting to observe that the 36 colleges paid 90% of the dues and were 68% of the institutional membership, and that the 17 seminaries, 32% of the institutional membership, paid 10% of the institutional dues.

Special mention should be made of the contributions received from the *Lutheran Brotherhood Insurance Society,* Minneapolis, to assist in the publishing of the proceedings of the annual meetings, the holding of the William's Bay Conference on "The Lutheran Church and Education," and for the encouragement in the Martin Luther Faculty Fellowship Program.

The Staff

Prior to 1958 the Conference never had a paid staff. The secretary and the treasurer were either a president or a professor of a member college and seminary, or a secretary of a member board of (higher) education. They performed their tasks on their spare time, if they had any, and utilized the secretarial service of the institution or board with which they were connected. Generally, even the postage for miscellaneous correspondence related to the office was paid by the institution or board, except in the mailing of the News Bulletin which was paid for on the basis of records carefully kept and invoices submitted annually to the Conference for approval. The Conference always expressed its appreciation for these services, although not fully aware of all that was involved. To these institutions and boards, as well as to the personnel involved, the Conference is greatly indebted for its existence from 1910 to 1958.

It is only just that some recognition be given to those who served as secretaries and treasurers, who might be considered as staff members, for they were the ones who really did most of the work, both in preparing program, directing the annual meetings and collecting the dues. The vice-presidents seldom rendered any special service, except to attend meetings of the executive committee and to preside at some sessions of the annual meetings.

The *secretaries* and the institutions or boards with which they were related were, as listed in chronological order: F. B. Sawvell, Thiel College, 1910; F. P. Manhart, Susquehanna University, 1911; C. T. Benze, Thiel College, 1912; H. D. Hoover, Carthage College, 1916-1921; R. E. Tulloss, Wittenberg College, 1922-1926; H. F. Martin, Midland College, 1927-1929; Gould Wickey, Board of Education, UCLA, 1930-1934; J. C. K. Preus, Board of Education, NLC., 1935; H. J. Arnold, Professor, Wittenberg College and later president Hartwick College, 1936-1941; 1946-1949; F. C. Wiegman, Midland College, 1942-1945; W. F. Zimmerman, Thiel College, 1950; W. P. Hieronymus, Midland College, 1951; Orville Dahl, Board of Education, ELC., 1952-1957; Gould Wickey, Board of Education, ULCA, 1958-59, and after retirement from the Board of Education, ULCA, served as secretary and executive director, 1960-

1966; and secretary 1967 under the new name of the Conference, namely, Lutheran Educational Conference of North America.

The office of *treasurer* was not established until 1912 when the name of Professor Martzoff appears (with no institution listed); Otto Mees, Capital University, 1916; J. Stump, professor, Chicago Lutheran Theological Seminary, 1918-1920; J. A. Aasgaard, Concordia College, Moorhead, Minn., 1921; H. J. Arnold, Professor, Wittenberg College, 1922-1941; and 1946-1949 as president, Hartwick College; F. C. Wiegman, Midland College, 1942-1945; W. F. Zimmerman, Thiel College, 1950; W. F. Hieronymus, Midland College, 1951; Orville Dahl, Board of Education, ELC., 1952-1957; Gould Wickey, Board of Education, ULCA., 1958-1959; A. Barbara Wiegand, Washington, D.C., 1960-1964; and Charles H. Solem, Washington, D.C., 1965-1967.

With the reorganization of the Conference in January 1958, provision was made for such dues as would be adequate for the employment of secretarial service, the renting of offices, obtaining necessary equipment and supplies, and employment of a part-time executive director.

Miss Gertrude Belser and Mrs. Henry Schumann did the basic work in developing the Placement Bureau. Several other persons were employed during the period, 1958-1966. Miss Ruth Peterson was the chief office secretary from December 1959 to January 31, 1967. For the efficient service of the office staff the Conference expressed its appreciation from year to year.

Gould Wickey was elected executive director on a part-time basis beginning February 1, 1958 and continued as such until January 31, 1967.

It is altogether proper to give recognition to those persons who served only as president or in some other office(s) but whose pictures were not obtained. They were presidents of their institutions unless otherwise stated.

Name of Person and his Institution	*Office and Date Held*
Aasgaard, J. A., Concordia College, Moorhead, Minn.	Treasurer, 1921 Vice-President, 1924
Benze, C. T., Thiel College, Greenville, Pa.	Secretary, 1912
Elson, H. W., Thiel College, Greenville, Pa.	Vice-President, 1921
Granville, W. A., Gettysburg College	President, 1919
Gullixon, T. F., Luther Seminary, St. Paul	Vice-President, 1921
Hanson, H. W. A., Gettysburg College,	President, 1935
Harms, J. Henry, Newberry College,	President, 1916
Heckert, C. G. Wittenberg College	President, 1912
Krueger, J. F., Midland College	President, 1924
Manhart, F. P., professor, Susquehanna University	Secretary, 1911

Martzoff, professor (initials and institution not given)	Treasurer, 1912
Nikander, V. K., Suomi College	Vice-President, 1940-41
Proehl, Otto, Wartburg College	Vice-President, 1931
Shatzer, C. G., Dean Wittenberg College	President, 1946
Solberg, C. O., Augustana College, (S.D.)	Vice-President, 1926
Stauffer, E. E., Midland College	President, 1921
Stump, J., professor, Chicago Lutheran Theol. Sem.	Treasurer, 1918-20
Tyson, L., Muhlenberg College	President, 1951
Wald, Arthur, Dean, Augustana College (Ill.)	Vice-President, 1935
Wargelin, J. Suomi College	Vice-President, 1934
Zimmerman, W. F. Thiel College	Secretary and Treasurer, 1950

Guiding Hands and Minds

Studying the minutes of the Conference, the work of committees, and the activities of individuals; reviewing the list of officers, the number of offices held and the years of service; and noting the list of speakers with the number of addresses delivered or papers presented, taking all these factors into consideration, it would seem that the Conference has been largely guided through its fifty-seven years of history by the hands and minds of the following persons, named alphabetically:

Gustave A. Andreen, Henry J. Arnold, Conrad Bergendoff, Orville Dahl, Frederick G. Gotwald, Clemens M. Granskou, John A. W. Haas, Harvey D. Hoover, O. P. Kretzmann, Mary E. Markley, Erland Nelson, Sidney Rand, C. C. Stoughton, Rees Edgar Tulloss, William L. Young, and Gould Wickey.

It is quite evident that some others, if they had been in Lutheran higher education, for a longer period of time and related to the Conference, would have their names added to the list.

L. A. Vigness
President, St. Olaf College
Northfield, Minn.
Secretary, Board of Education,
Norwegian Lutheran Church
NLEC
Vice-President, 1919
President, 1920

G. A. Andreen
President, Augustana College
Rock Island, Ill.
NLEC
Vice-President, 1916, 1930
President, 1918, 1926

Otto Mees
President, Capital University
Columbus, Ohio
NLEC
President, 1923

L. W. Boe
President, St. Olaf College
Northfield, Minn.
NLEC
President, 1925

ACTIVE AS OFFICERS AND ON MANY COMMITTEES

Rees Edgar Tulloss, Ph.D.
President, Wittenberg, College
Springfield, Ohio
NLEC
Secretary, 1922-1926
President, 1927

H. J. Arnold, Ph.D.
Professor, Wittenberg College
and later
President, Hartwick College
Oneonta, N.Y.
NLEC
Treasurer, 1921-1941
President, 1942-1944
Vice-President, 1945
Secretary-Treasurer, 1946, 1949

CHAPTER II
Problems and Areas of Concern

The problems and areas of concern to be mentioned in this chapter are not so much the problems and concerns of the Conference *qua* Conference but rather the problems and concerns of the educational institutions and the church bodies which support these institutions. The Conference seemed more interested in the problems of the member schools than in its own particular problems, at least the minutes and the records do not discuss what were considered the basic problems of the Conference as a Conference. Only casually is there mentioned the matter of the finances of the Conference. The chief problems of the Conference were not lack of interest of the personnel of its member schools nor the willingness to attend meetings even at great distances with considerable expenditure of time and money.

The chief problems of the Conference related to its own existence and effectiveness were the lack of funds to do what should have been done and the lack of personnel to give continuous attention to the problems and concerns of the educational institutions. The use of presidents and professors with full-time duties in their own institutions did not allow for the attention to programs of service which the Conference should have rendered in the 1920s. This situation was not explicitly stated until 1958, when Dr. Orville Dahl, the secretary, frankly declared his opinion. Mention is made of this in the first Chapter in the section under Reorganization. Until 1958 it seems as though the Conference was not willing to attempt a particular service other than holding an annual meeting and obtaining the benefit of various studies and surveys which generally professors and sometimes presidents were willing to make. However, a stab was made at getting more teachers for Lutheran schools. Special mention of these studies and surveys is made in chapter III. It seems to this writer that the chief problem of the Conference as an organization was to obtain some one who could give the desired attention to and leadership in a program of service. It was only through the volunteered service of the executive of the Board of Education, UCLA, that a News Bulletin was started.

The problems and areas of concern to be noted in this chapter are those manifested in the papers and addresses presented at the annual meetings, in the special resolutions approved at the various meetings, in the research projects, the studies and the surveys, and in some special events.

A. As Seen in the Papers and Addresses presented at Annual Meetings

It appears that a general subject or theme was not used for the annual meetings until 1933, at least such is not recorded in the minutes or the printed programs. Sometimes papers are listed and the authors were not present and the papers were not read, but at times the authors sent the papers which were read by an appointed person, frequently the secretary.

To indicate the range of interest and concern, the papers have been categorized under some seventeen topics. The list could have been more extensive. Until 1936 many of the subjects were categorized under more than one topic. It was not deemed necessary for the purpose of this documentary history to continue this cross-indexing. There would be differences of opinion as to both the topics to be cross-indexed and the selection of the cross-indexed topic. This list of papers thus arranged under categories is included in the following pages.

The papers read at the annual meetings are also arranged under an alphabetical list of the authors together with the years when the papers were presented. This list is added to this chapter as an appendix.

Since no papers were printed until 1919 and none from 1942 to and including 1959, it was not thought desirable and it was not possible on the basis of the time-table, to study the contents of the papers. Some student searching for a subject for a master's and even a doctor's degree might find such a study of interest and value, especially as indicative of the sign of the times, of their possible effect on changes in college and seminary curricula, and of the significance for the church and country.

Papers and Addresses Arranged under Categories
with titles, authors, and dates when presented

An asterisk (*) indicates the topic is listed also under another category. This system of cross-indexing was not followed after 1936, even though many titles deserve such cross-indexing. R.T. indicates Round Table. There is not consistency in the programs in recording the names of those who participated in a Round Table discussion. Sometimes the minutes do not record them; sometimes the number of persons participating is of such size that it would have made the listing cumbersome and of little historical value.

Alphabetical List of Categories

1. Academy, Preparatory School—Church, Christian
2. Bible
3. Christian (Religious) Education—General and Higher
4. Church and Education in Other Countries
5. Church Board of Education
6. Church, State and Education (Culture)
7. College—Church, Christian
8. Historical—review and preview; Organizational
9. Lutheran Church
10. Lutheran Higher Education
11. Ministry, Ministerial Candidates

12. Miscellaneous
13. Publicity and Promotion
14. Student
15. Teacher, Faculty
16. Theological Seminary—Ministerial Training
17. Work With Lutheran Students at Non-Lutheran Schools

1. Academy, Preparatory School—Church, Christian

The Lutheran Preparatory School	J. L. Kistler	1910
The Academy and High School as Sources of Supply	O. F. Bert	1911
Preparatory Schools	A. H. Arbaugh	1912
The Church Secondary School: Scope, Service, Support	M. Hegland	1919
The Church Academy in Light of Norwegian America	O. M. Norlie	1925

2. Bible

A Factor in Higher Education	P. S. Vig	1920
The Lutheran Bible School	O. Ingvoldstad	1920
Survey of Bible Teaching and Allied Subjects in Lutheran and non-Lutheran Colleges and Secondary Schools	P. H. Heisey O. Bostrom H. F. Martin	1923
Bible Knowledge of College Students *	J. F. Krueger	1925
Bible as Literature and in Literature	C. Ackerman	1926
The English Bible and the Teacher of English	G. H. Hartwig	1938

3. Christian (Religious) Education—General and Higher

A Course of Training for General Religious Work	H. D. Hoover	1912
Religious Education	C. S. Bauslin	1921
Religious Education in Modern Church	M. H. Krumbine	1922
Week-Day Religious Education, Challenge to College	H. S. Bechtold	1922
Religious Education in Program of Colleges and Seminaries	S. G. Hefelbower	1924
Religious Education in Lutheran Colleges	F. W. Kroencke	1934
Luther and Christian Education	J. F. Krueger	1934
Evangelism—A Challenge to Christian Higher Education	E. Nelson	1935
The Oxford Conference on Life and Work and its Implications for Christian Education	C. Bergendoff	1938
Current Issues in Christian Higher Education	G. Wickey	1948

4. Church and Education In Other Countries

5. Church Board of Education

6. Church, State and Education (Culture)

The Spiritual Foundations of Freedom	B. Christensen	1942
The Christian Church and Democracy		1940
(Panel: J. C. Kinard, N. R. Melhorn, T. F. Gullixson E. B. Lawson, O. Mees)		
Church-State Relations in Education		1962
1. From the Point of View of Catholicism	F. G. Hochwalt	
2. From the Point of View of Protestantism	A. G. Huegli	
Creative Tensions: Church and Government		1964
Speakers: Honorable B. Hays and George Forell		
Christianity and Culture	K. E. Mattson	1964

7. College: Church, Christian

Educational Standards of Denominational Colleges	J. A. Singmaster	1910
The Advantages of Combined Academic and Industrial Courses	E. M. Stahl	1910
How Harmonize Christian Ideals and Modern Educational Standards in a College Curriculum	J. A. Morehead	1911
Some Problems of College Government	J. H. Harms	1911
The Social Life of the Church College	J. P. Schneider	1912
The Advantages of Courses in Music, Art, Domestic Science, etc. in our Colleges	J. L. Van Gundy	1912
Co-Education	C. T. Benze	1912
Honorary Degrees	F. P. Manhart	1912
Financing the Church College	R. B. Peery	1912
What Graduate Work is Advisable in our Colleges	G. T. Ettinger	1912
What Constitutes a Christian College Education	J. A. Morehead	1916
What Can the Colleges do to Win and Conserve Ministerial Candidates	E. H. Krauss	1916
What Can Colleges Contribute toward the Success of the 1917 Quadri-centennial	V. G. A. Tressler	1916
Task of the Christian College in War-time	R. B. Peery	1918
What Should be the Attitude of our Lutheran Colleges toward the Movement to Abolish Latin as a Requisite for the A.B. Degree	G. A. Andreen	1918
How to Raise Money for Colleges	H. D. Hoover	1918
The Church College and Its Alumni	C. J. Bengston	1919
Reorganization of the Church College	J. A. Morehead	1919
Federal Supervision of Higher Education	H. W. Elson	1919

51

8. Historical—Reviews and Previews and Organizational

9. The Lutheran Church

11. Ministerial Candidates—The Ministry

12. Miscellaneous

13. Publicity and Promotion

14. Student

15. Teachers, Faculty, Teaching

16. Theological Seminary—Ministerial Training

Analysis of the Book, "A Study of Theological
  Education in America"
  by Niebuhr, Williams, Gustafson   RT   1957
Same Subject as 1957   RT   1958
Basic Principles of Curriculum Construction
  for Theological Education   W. Wolbrecht   1959
Welfare Provision in the Seminary   A. Rogness   1959
Financial Subsidy for Seminaries from Busi-
  ness, etc.   C. C. Stoughton   1959
Some Standards of the AATS   A. H. Ewald   1959
The Responsibility of Seminaries
  Relevant Findings of the Study of Theologi-
    cal Education   D. Williams   1960
    (Panel: D. Heiges, E. C. Fendt, K. E. Mattson, A. N. Rogness,
                     W. Wolbrecht)
Constructive Changes in Theological Educa-
  tion   1960
  The Place of the Teacher   J. H. Ziegler
  Implication of the Pre-Seminary Study   D. W. Culver
  Reshaping Seminary Curricula   W. Lazareth
  Relationships in the Seminary   D. M. Rhoads
Articulation between Liberal Arts Colleges and
  Seminaries in the Education of Persons for
  the Ministry and other Church Occupations   1961
  1. In their Selection   V. L. Strempke
  2. In their Motivation   A. H. Becker
The Eschatological Aspect of Today's Theo-
logical Curriculum   1961
  (Panel: B. Christensen, J. Reumann, K.
          Mattson, C. S. Meyer)
Theology for Everyman   1962
  Presentations: A. H. Ewald, D. W. Stough-
          ton, C. L. Taylor
Developments in Theological Education   K. R. Bridston   1963
  —Preliminary Findings in Requirements for
  Entrance into Seminaries
Arrangements for Lutheran Theological Edu-
  cation   1964
  Reporters: C. Bergendoff, E. C. Fendt, A.
          O. Fuerbringer
Feasibility of a Pan-Lutheran Consultation on
  the Role of Theological Education in the
  Church Today   V. R. Westlund

17. Work with Lutheran Students at Non-Lutheran Schools

E. J. BRAULICK
President, Wartburg College
Waverly, Iowa
NLEC
Vice-President, 1938
President, 1939

J. C. K. PREUS
*Executive Secretary, Board of Chris-
tain Education*
Norwegian Lutheran Church
NLEC
President, 1932
Secretary, 1935

W. P. HIERONYMUS, Ph.D.
President, Midland College,
Fremont, Nebraska
NLEC
Vice-President, 1929, 1947
President, 1948
Secretary-Treasurer, 1951

C. H. BECKER
President, Wartburg College
Waverly, Iowa
NLEC
Vice-President, 1953
President, 1954

B. As Seen in Special Resolutions

In this section are placed copies of the more important resolutions passed or considered by the Conference during its fifty-seven year history. They are listed under categories with the dates when considered. This arrangement will help to point out the significance of some resolutions, especially as to the time when presented. Sometimes, a special report will be noted which was received but there was no definite resolution of approval. In some instances, this author makes comments which help to understand the import of the subject under consideration. We have tried to include all the important resolutions but all such recorded resolutions may not be considered significant by other persons.

The categories under which the resolutions are listed are not necessarily mutually exclusive. A somewhat shorter list of categories might have been used but the variety of resolutions would not have been evident so easily. The following is the list of categories used:

1. Academic Items
2. Bible Teaching in the Curriculum
3. Colleges
4. Educational Year
5. Faculty, Teachers
6. Lutheran Higher Education
7. Lutheran Literature and Authorship
8. Lutheran Unity and Cooperation
9. Ministerial Education
10. Miscellaneous
11. News Bulletin
12. Organization and Membership
13. Other Groups and Organizations
14. Placement Bureau, Teachers' Directory
15. Prizes, Scholarships, Fellowships
16. Public Relations: Promotion and Publicity
17. Seminaries, Theological
18. Students . . . Campus Ministry

1. Academic Items

1910—Entrance requirements

That we recommend that entrance requirements be no lower than those of other standard institutions in the section in which a Lutheran Institution is located.

—Courses to prepare for technical studies

That courses be provided by our colleges that will prepare students to enter upon technical courses of study.

70

—Hours per week

That the number of hours of class instructions for college professors be 16 hours per week as a maximum.

1912—Regarding honorary degrees

With reference to honorary degrees, it is the judgment in this Conference that the recommendations for the honorary degree originate in the faculty of the colleges.

1923—Report of a survey commission

The commission reported that it had worked out a division of the general field to investigate (1) general relationship, service and aims; (2) equipment, endowment and incomes; and (3) faculty, curriculum and student activities. The commission reported that questionnaires had been completed and would be submitted for criticism and final approval. The commission believed that such a survey

1. Will furnish a definite body of information which can be used by college executives in a study of their administrative problems, and which can be used as a guide in working out their expansion programs.

2. Will indicate both the strength and weakness of the Lutheran educational institutions in this country.

3. Will in some measure at least determine a set of minimum standards for Lutheran educational institutions.

4. Will provide for college executives who wish to use it for that purpose a definite statement of the urgent needs of the institution which can be used in presenting these needs to individuals, boards and bodies throughout the Church and to the larger philanthropic agencies.

5. Will increase respect for us on the part of non-Lutheran institutions.

1926—Extension courses

That we favor Extension Courses where they are feasible, and under the condition that standards be not lowered, nor the efficiency of professors impaired by too heavy a teaching load.

—Critical study of curricula

That we suggest to our colleges and theological seminaries: (1) a critical study of their curricula, and (2) a study of the function and the methods of a Lutheran college or seminary in its efforts to meet the demands of the present in equipping men for the ministry in the fullest measure possible.

1931—Higher scholastic standards

The National Lutheran Educational Conference, mindful of the significance and value to our Lutheran colleges and seminaries, of many of the newer findings relating to educational principles, more effective administrative and teaching techniques, Resolves:

1. That this conference commend and endorse the legitimate scientific efforts now being put forth to raise scholastic standards, improve administrative and teaching techniques, and to make more effective the various contacts between the student and institution.

2. That we as an educational conference encourage and foster in our colleges and seminaries experimental studies designed to lead to improved methods of teaching, higher standards of student achievement and more efficient administrative procedures.

3. That this conference authorize the appointment of an educational research committee of five or more representatives of Lutheran colleges and seminaries to inaugurate such experimental studies for the ensuing year as may be found desirable to undertake.

4. That the report of this committee be given a place on the 1932 program of the conference.

   —*Correlation of College and Seminary Curricula*

In view of changing conditions in our collegiate institutions, due to the elective system, the Committee is of the opinion that one of three things is required:

1. That the colleges give larger attention to the specific needs of men preparing to enter a theological school, or

2. That seminaries change their requirements to meet the changed curricula of the colleges, or

3. That the seminaries extend their curricula in order to impart both the theological instruction necessary also to compensate for the omission of certain studies during the collegiate years which are considered essential to a theological education.

2. Bible Teaching, Biblical Subjects in Curricula

1924—A declaration that faith in the Holy Word and the divinity of the Saviour must underly all instruction at educational institutions of the Lutheran Church.

Whereas, There is threatening Protestantism today a serious schism on the question of faith in the Revealed Word of God, and in the Deity of our Lord, Jesus Christ; and

Whereas, Much of the genesis of this controversy lies in the teaching of some colleges and seminaries which question the divine authority of the Word;

Therefore, Be it resolved, That we, the National Lutheran Educational Conference, hereby go on record as reaffirming our faith in Holy Scriptures as the divine and infallible rule of faith and life, and in Jesus Christ as true God and true man, and as the only all-powerful Saviour and

Redeemer; and

That this faith underlies and shall continue to underlie all the instruction in our academies, colleges, and theological seminaries.

1925—Attitude toward the Christian Religion

A committee appointed to survey the Universities of the country with reference to their attitude toward the Christian Religion made a report indicating great difficulties in the way of the project, and *requested that the Committee be discharged.*

1926—Teaching of the Bible

Resolved, that in the teaching of the Bible, we consider the emphasis on the spiritual content the essential feature.

3. Colleges

1923—Commission on Survey of Lutheran Colleges

This is noted under the category of Academic Items.

1926—Tuition Rates

That, observing the greatly decreased purchasing power of the dollar, with the consequent increased financial burden upon our educational institutions, and recognizing the propriety of asking that those who enjoy the benefits of these institutions shall share in the increased cost of operation, it is the sense of the National Lutheran Education Conference that a tuition fee of $200 per year may properly be regarded as an appropriate minimum in our four-year Lutheran Colleges.

1932—Firm Faith in the Liberal Arts College

That this Association express its firm faith in the Liberal Arts College as an important and indispensable factor in the educational field. The Church dare not omit or fail to emphasize the value of the Liberal Arts College for the training of Church leadership.

1933—Several resolutions were approved at this meeting, which concerned the colleges but they are noted under Lutheran Higher Education and Lutheran Literature and Authorship and Research.

1957—College in California

Whereas, it is desirable and urgent to increase our witness potential in the area of higher education, as in other phases of our Church's work;

Whereas, the growth in population, business, industry, education, and the Church's work in California has been truly remarkable and most significant for the future of our Church;

Therefore, Be It Resolved,

That the NLEC looks with favor upon the survey now in process by educational representatives of The American Lutheran Church, The Augustana Lutheran Church, The Evangelical Lutheran Church, and The United Lutheran Church in America, seeking to determine the feasibility of establishing a Lutheran four-year college of liberal arts in California.

—Prepare for Larger Enrollment

Whereas, enrollments at colleges and universities during the next fifteen years will probably increase from 80 to 100 percent; and

Whereas, the Lutheran Church has a responsibility to its own youth who desire and are capable of pursuing a college education; and

Whereas, Christian higher education is a distinct need in American higher education;

Therefore, Be It Resolved,

That the NLEC (a) calls upon Lutheran Colleges to plan a very substantial increase with special attention to more Lutheran students; and (b) urges Lutheran bodies to recognize their responsibility in higher education by significantly increasing their grants to colleges during the years ahead; and (c) that copies of this Resolution be transmitted to the officials of the various Lutheran bodies, to the Boards of Christian higher education, and to the Chairmen of the Boards of the various member colleges.

4. Educational Year and Campaigns

1911—Committee Appointed

That, in view of the urgency of the educational situation, a committee of three be appointed to consider the feasibility of, and plans for, an active and general campaign throughout our Church in America in behalf of Christian education and to report at our next meeting.

(Drs. Gotwald, Gongaware, and Schuh were appointed)

1927—Educational Year approved

That we have learned with satisfaction of the progress which has been made during the year toward the realization of the project of simultaneous campaigns on the part of all Lutheran educational institutions throughout the country during the year of 1930, the 400th anniversary of the Augsburg Confession.

We commend the action of the United Lutheran Church in setting aside the year 1930 as "educational year" in that body. We note with pleasure the messages of approval of the general project from various persons in the different branches of the Church.

In view of these evidences of a favorable reaction toward the proposal, Be It Resolved,

That we express ourselves as being in hearty approval with the holding of a series of simultaneous campaigns during the year 1930, on the part of all Lutheran educational institutions, each to appeal in its own way, in its own field, to its own constituency.

In cases where for some reason a financial campaign during 1930 is not practicable, special emphasis should be given to the cause of Christian education.

We urge consideration of this proposal by the general church bodies and synods related to our various schools, in the hope that by simultaneous campaigns and combined emphasis upon educational needs during 1930, the cause of education and the welfare of our schools may be largely furthered.

1928—Progress in plans for Educational Year

(1) That we have noted with deep satisfaction the further progress which has been made in the development of plans for the observance of 1930 as Educational Year throughout all branches of the Lutheran Church in America.

(2) That we appoint a special committee consisting of President R. E. Tulloss, President G. A. Andreen, President O. C. Mees and President L. W. Boe to arrange for an early meeting of college presidents and representatives of Lutheran Church bodies for discussion of this project, to the end that by campaigns or other emphasis the cause of Christian education in our Lutheran colleges, academies, and seminaries throughout America may be stressed during the year named.

1928—Informal meeting of representatives of Lutheran Synods and educational institutions.

On March 14, 1928 there was an informal meeting of representatives of various Lutheran synods and Lutheran educational institutions at Hotel Sherman, Chicago, Ill. President R. E. Tulloss was elected Chairman of the meeting and President J. N. Brown secretary. Dr. Tulloss said the purpose of the conference was to plan for some united action on the part of all Lutheran educational institutions for the raising of funds and for the awakening of interest in Christian education, all of which has been discussed on various occasions, especially at meetings of the National Lutheran Educational Conference.

The reasons for such a campaign was stated as 1) the continued need notwithstanding progress; 2) mutual benefits to the schools; and 3) gain for the church.

It was recognized that there would be and are difficulties such as: achieving simultaneous effort; recent campaigns have been staged for many institutions; the time will not be opportune in some sections; some will fear unionism; opposition will be encountered from other causes; some are tired of educational campaigns; some will dread the work involved.

A continuation committee was appointed, of which President Tulloss was to be a member. The function of this committee was to stimulate further interest and activity with reference to the educational emphases and campaigns in 1930; to cooperate with the National Lutheran Educational Conference in handling various related matters; and to convene educational representatives of various institutions and church bodies for further conference.

5. Faculty, Teachers

1925—Teachers with religious convictions

That this Convention recognize with strongest approbation the present general practice in our Lutheran institutions of employing only preceptors of positive religious convictions and influence.

We recommend that as far as possible our teachers be chosen from among the active members of the Lutheran Church.

1929—Exchange of professors

That we favor the idea of exchange of professors, believing it to be for the mutual welfare of both teachers and institutions.

1957—To seek qualified and committed teachers

Whereas, there is a clearly recognized continuing and growing need for qualified and committed teachers in our Lutheran colleges; and

Whereas, every laudable effort should be made to increase the supply as expeditiously as possible; therefore,

Be It Resolved, that the following specific techniques be used without undue delays

a) That the faculties in our various colleges be urged to set up committees specifically charged with the responsibility of discovering and encouraging talented undergraduates to prepare themselves for teaching in our Lutheran colleges.

b) That the NLEC encourage the Boards of Higher Education of the respective Lutheran church bodies to invest larger sums of money in the educating of Lutheran men and women for positions on the faculties of both seminaries and colleges.

c) That, as soon as possible, the Placement Bureau expand its services by establishing a department for the pooling of information about prospective college and seminary teachers, it being understood that the necessary financial support would have to be equitably shared.

1959—Excellence in teaching

That this Conference urges all participating members to pursue well-planned studies on the theme of this meeting. The Christian Teacher—Channel of Excellence, with its implications for the faculty, the students and the administration, and that the Executive Committee initiate such guidance and directives as will provide necessary materials for the above duties.

That the Conference expresses its conviction on the importance of the Christian teacher achieving the desired excellence in Christian education. This conviction is prompted by:

a. The great need for Christian teachers;
b. The necessity of providing opportunities for the continued personal and professional growth of Christian teachers; and
c. The crucial urgency of immediate financial resources for increasing and developing Christian faculties for today's educational world.

1960—Exchange of faculty with Andhra Christian College

That the Conference request the Executive Committee and Executive Director to consider the possibility of an exchange of faculty members with the Andhra Christian College in India and other educational institutions abroad, and the possibility of arranging a third-year program in the Andhra Christian College for students from our institutions in America.

(This suggestion was not approved by the boards of World Missions of the various Lutheran Church bodies, nor by the Executive Committee.)

6. Lutheran Higher Education

1911—Committee Appointed

That a Committee of three be appointed to consider a plan for the unification of Lutheran higher education. (Drs. Tressler, Harms and Schuh appointed).

1919—National Lutheran University

Whereas, the Lutheran Church so designated has been born in a University and has ever since maintained and championed the verse 'Ye shall know the Truth and the Truth shall make you free' as a necessary supplement to that other verse 'The just shall live by faith', and whereas there is in our country no great Central University from which may radiate throughout the length and breadth of our beloved land the principles of the truth as we confess it,

Therefore, Be It Resolved, That the National Lutheran Educational Conference in joint session assembled at Chicago, in the year of our Lord 1919, earnestly petition the Lutherans of these United States to pray that our Heavenly Father may appoint the way whereby an effectual door may be opened and a National Lutheran University of approved scholarship be founded for the education of men and women of high ideals and advanced standing, and for the dissemination of the truth as we confess it throughout our land.

1933—Towards boards' support

That the various colleges and seminaries, in conference with the boards of education through their executive secretaries, define as clearly as possible their respective objectives, and that the boards give their vigorous support by helping them severally to carry out their distinctive programs by means of publicity, economic encouragement, and practical counsel.

—Towards spiritual values and sound social skills.

That in the face of the present world disorder, in the face of the findings of the committee appointed three years ago by President Hoover to study conditions, we request our colleges to study diligently the ways and means by which to inculcate more effectually a deeper grip on spiritual values, and a more effective participation in sound social skills.

1935—A Seminar in Lutheran Higher Education

That this Conference recognizes the value to the Lutheran Higher Education of the work done by the Lutheran Seminar at the University of Chicago in the summer of 1933, and gives its moral support and encouragement to similar efforts in the future.

1953—Private, Independent, Christian higher education

That as representatives of the Lutheran Church and as a group specifically interested in the education of the youth of our land, we express our sincere conviction that private, independent, and Christian educational activities and institutions are a living part of our American tradition, and that the continuance of such private, independent, and Christian activities and institutions is a necessary and integral part pf the democratic structure of our nation. We view with alarm developments which tend to destroy such institutions and we wish to alert our constituencies to the dangers of a situation in which a proper balance between public and private education is not maintained. Through our secretary we ask the Boards of Education of the bodies represented in the NLEC to make this a subject of special study. We ask the executive committee to initiate further studies during the coming year and to place this subject on the agenda at the next meeting of the NLEC.

1953—Division of Higher Education in National Lutheran Council

Whereas, it has been proposed that study be made of the advisability of including in the structure of the National Lutheran Council a Division of Higher Education; therefore, Be It Resolved: That this subject be included in the agenda for the next meeting of the NLEC.

1962—Regarding a Philosophy of Lutheran Education

1. That the Executive Board of this Conference appoint a special com-

mittee to cooperate with the individual boards of higher education to study the philosophy of Lutheran education, and, in due time, to prepare a volume on the principles and objectives of Lutheran higher education in the United States and Canada, and

2. That in commending this research this Conference recognizes its responsibility to urge its affiliated boards of education and/or some foundation(s) to support the project with ample funds.

That this resolution be referred to the Executive Board for study and report at the next annual meeting.

(Note: This resolution stimulated the action which resulted in the Lake Geneva Conference. See section C in chapter III.)

1963—Possible Cooperative Projects

Whereas, national and international developments offer opportunities and imply responsibilities for higher education which are not adequately cared for by programs and policies under the jurisdiction of individual institutions, and

Whereas, the National Lutheran Educational Conference is the only inclusive agency of (Lutheran) institutions of higher education,

Therefore, Be It Resolved, That the Executive Director and the officers of the NLEC consider ways in which we might effectively engage in cooperative projects and to that end confer with Boards of Higher Education of our respective church bodies.

1964—Lutheran Higher Education and World Understanding

That the study-report of the Executive Director on Lutheran Higher Education and International Understanding be transmitted to each member institution for such study and implementation as may be deemed advisable.

That each member institution appoint a Committee of Faculty and Students to study and recommend to the faculty what the institution might undertake, recognizing that the president should exercise desirable leadership in the matter.

That the executives of the respective boards of college and theological education consider with their respective institutions the feasibility of projects in the area of international understanding and service.

That each Lutheran college explore the possibilities of having some sort of a study program abroad whether separately or cooperatively.

That the NLEC act as a coordinator and distributor of information in the field of international understanding and service.

(Note: Some schools have developed study programs abroad, and more are being planned. To what extent this study-report has been a factor in stimulating such study-abroad programs, no attempt has been made to ascertain.)

7. Lutheran Literature and Authorship

1922—A report of the Commission on Lutheran Literature

It is a well-known fact that our Church is not taking her just place in American Christianity in the sphere of scholarly publications and literature. There is a lack of systematic plans in developing scholars, and in using them and keeping them connected with the life of our church. We are not making our position clear, nor establishing the truth we are called to defend among thinking men and women. What we ought to give American Christianity in thoughtful presentation of truth is not being given. In view of this situation your Commission asks the Lutheran Educational Conference to awaken the Church to this deplorable condition, and to propose the following remedies:

1. Our Institutions of learning should labor to produce more scholars of the highest type. It is the special duty of our colleges to seek out men of promise and to endeavor to keep them closely tied to the church during their university career. Our theological seminaries should strive not only to train practical pastors, but also to develop scholarly students among the lines of their strongest talents and equipment for future theological leadership.

2. The Church should be aroused to provide adequate funds so that our colleges and seminaries can secure and retain some professors who shall give themselves less to teaching than to thorough research and worthy publication of careful and scientifically valuable results.

3. Provision should be made to discover and encourage more writers, and to secure the highest type of books through adequate prizes offered by our Church Boards of Publication.

4. In our judgment there is need of a distinctively Christian point of view, which should permeate books of the best standard in psychology, ethics, philosophy, history, economics, sociology, and the natural sciences, In theology we ought to show productive scholarship of the best sort in content and form to cover every department of theology.

5. We express it as our opinion that the Church Boards of Publication should expend part of the profits made through the sale of Church books, Sunday School and popular literature, upon the publication of scholarly books, which do not pay. Men of ability should be sought out and adequately compensated to produce the kind of scholarly literature in which our Church should be represented, and through which she ought to endeavor to conquer all learning for Christ.

1933—To encourage authorship

That it is the sense of this conference that our schools aim towards making distinctive contributions to scholarship, that they encourage authorship, and that our colleges include among their definite objectives to foster authoritative scholarship in such fields as are peculiarly adapted to the genius of the Lutheran Church. That, with the return of better economic conditions, our colleges endeavor to endow fields of special research, both as an encouragement to our men of ability to stay with us and make their contributions within our group, and at the same time thus to claim and achieve the status and prestige in the field of learning that of right belongs to us.

8. Lutheran Unity and Cooperation

1929—Promotion of unity

It was moved to continue with the discussion of the Promotion of Unity among the Synods of the Church, in view of the fact that the NLEC has been making every effort to secure better acquaintance and better cooperation among general bodies of Lutherans and stands in a position to foster such relations.

1935—Some conditions for Lutheran unity

The discussion brought forth the unity which now exists amongst the various Lutheran groups such as a common confession, attitude to the Word of God, and Hymnology; a cooperation in Foreign Missions, Home Missions and Inner Missions. It was suggested that the Lutheran unity of the future depends on:

1. An interpretation of past history recognizing that the statements of the fathers are sign-posts not hitching-posts.
2. An adequate presentation of the facts of the present situation with the attitude of appreciation and less criticism.
3. A larger acquaintance with one another.
4. The forward look with reconstruction of the pattern of the Church which has been spoiled by men.
5. The spirit of sacrifice for the larger good.

9. Ministerial Education

1924—An Extract from a letter from Professor D. D. Leib, Connecticut College.

The following is an interesting extract from a letter from Professor Leib, read by the secretary at the Conference:

"I confess to a great desire to hear or know what is said about 'Desirable College Courses for Students expecting to Enter our Seminaries.' I trust there is no feeling that the college courses of such should be confined or largely restricted to History, Philosophy, Languages, etc., i.e., such courses as could be regarded as necessary or desirable pre-requisites to the usual Seminary courses. The *educated* minister, (and the Lutheran Church believes in the educated ministry) should be able to think clearly in the fields of science, business and finance as well as in theology and exegesis. He should be familiar with economic laws as well as the laws of Moses. In short, his college education should be as broad as possible without being superficial, to furnish a proper background for his seminary course and his life work."

1925—Study of seminary curricula

That the Conference recommend the appointment of a Committee to continue the study of the curricula of our Theological Seminaries, submitting the results of the same to the faculties of our various seminaries, and reporting the results at the next Convention of this Conference.

10. Miscellaneous

1918—American University Union; Office in Paris

President J. A. Morehead suggested that the Conference consider the advisability and feasibility of opening a bureau in the American University Union in Paris. The Conference directed its secretary to communicate with the National Lutheran War Commission for Soldiers' and Sailors' Welfare with reference to the opening of such a bureau.

1919—American University Union

President Morehead reported that the opening of a Bureau for all Lutheran Institutions in the American University Union headquarters in Paris was found to be impracticable. Institutions represented in the Conference are invited to become members of the Union. The Union promises to be permanent.

1951—Universal Military Training

Whereas UMT is a controversial question and its realization would deeply affect American life in many fateful ways; and

Whereas, the manpower needs of the nation are being met by the Selective Service System which may be continued during the present emergency;

Therefore, Be It Resolved, That the NLEC is opposed to the introduction of UMT in the uncertain time when the total defense needs of our country can be so vaguely foreseen, and that we therefore urge the defeat of the proposal currently before the Congress of the United States.

—Regarding the gravity of the present crisis

The National Lutheran Educational Conference recognizes the gravity of the present crisis in world affairs and the great responsibilities it imposes upon our constituent institutions. The situation requires the fullest measure of devotion on the part of all Americans everywhere if our heritage of freedom is to be retained and our country to be preserved.

Therefore, Be It Resolved, that

1. It calls upon all its members—their faculties and student bodies—to

join before the Throne of Grace in ardent prayer that God may in His wisdom avert another world conflict and preserve our heritage of freedom for our children and our children's children.

2. It implores the blessing of Almighty God upon our national leaders that they may be endowed with wisdom and strength to keep our nation and the world in paths of peace.

3. It pledges the unqualified support of its members to a sound program of national preparedness.

4. It expresses the sincere conviction that in this time of national emergency our essential American freedom must be safeguarded both with respect to individual and to our religious, social and educational institutions.

5. It pledges it support for any program for the utilization of our manpower which will protect the national welfare and preserve our American heritage of freedom under God to the highest possible degree.

6. It pledges that whatever sacrifices may be required, we shall face the future with profound faith and unshaken confidence.

Out of these days of strain and stress, it is our solemn purpose that our institutions shall emerge richer and better equipped to measure up to their high trust as builders of men and women who will take their places as builders in a new world.

7. It asks the continuing prayer of the entire Lutheran Church in America for our nation, our Churches, and our educational institutions so that the Gospel may have free course and leaders of tomorrow may be trained for greater service to God and country.

1965—Lutheran-Roman Catholic Theological Conversations

That the National Lutheran Educational Conference agrees to sponsor conversations between Lutheran and Roman Catholic theologians, and

That the National Lutheran Educational Conference ask its Committee on Seminaries to function in this matter, contingent upon the formation of a similar Committee by the Catholic Commission for Ecumenical Relations.

It is understood (1) that the National Lutheran Council will support this project financially in an amount up to $1,500 annually, as reported by Dr. Paul Empie, and (2) that Dr. Paul Empie, executive director, National Lutheran Council, and the Rev. Virgil Westlund, secretary of the Department of Theological Cooperation, Division of Lutheran World Federation Affairs, be Advisory Members of the Committee on Seminaries of the NLEC.

After remarks by Dr. Empie and the clarification of the question that this action does not interfere with any conversations which may be held by Lutherans and Roman Catholic Theologians on a local basis,

IT WAS UNANIMOUSLY APPROVED.

It was voted, that the Committee on Seminaries be composed of Dr.

A. O. Fuerbringer, Concordia Seminary, St. Louis Mo.
Dr. Alvin Rogness, Lutheran Seminary, St. Paul, Minn. and
Dr. E. Theodore Bachmann, Board of Theological Education, Lutheran Church in America, the latter to function as chairman.

> (*Note*: Although the National Lutheran Council asked the National Lutheran Educational Conference to assume responsibility for these ecumenical conversations, and the Conference agreed appointing the above Committee, the Committee did not need to function. Suddenly, for some reason, it was determined that the Department of Theological Cooperation, Division of Lutheran World Affairs, National Lutheran Council should function in such matters.)

11. News Bulletin

1922—Need of a News Bulletin

Your secretary feels there is room for a mimeographed monthly news bulletin about what our institutions are doing.

1923—Cooperation of Lutheran Bureau, NLC.

That the Lutheran Bureau of the National Lutheran Council be requested to send out at such stated intervals as the Bureau may deem necessary, a mimeographed report of news items of the various colleges and seminaries which are members of this Association.

1924—Special Committee Appointed.

A motion was carried that a special committee consider the problem of the publication of a periodical devoted to the interests of Lutheran Educational Institutions, and of Lutheran teachers in Lutheran and non-Lutheran Schools.

(The officers were constituted this Committee and were given power to act with the proviso that they make no arrangements which would in any way involve the Conference financially.)

(It was suggested that "The Lutheran Survey" would perhaps be willing to set aside a certain number of pages in each issue for the use of the Conference.)

1932—Report of Committee adopted.

We commend as valuable and desirable, a Lutheran Educational News Bulletin. We recommend that a working agreement with the News Bulletin of the National Lutheran Council be sought, whereby the cooperation of as many as possible of our educational institutions may be enlisted and the Bulletin be given a proportionately wide distribution. We recommend that the officers of the Association be granted power to act in the matter.

12. Organization and Membership

1910—Boards' Secretaries as associate members

That the secretaries of the educational boards of church bodies represented be elected associate members of the Educational Conference.

—Western Schools asked to hold conference

That we suggest to our western theological seminaries, colleges and academies, to hold an educational conference, and that we look forward to a general conference which shall comprise all of the educational institutions of the Lutheran Church in America.

1911—Plan for permanent organization

That a committee of three be appointed at this meeting by the Chair, to present at our next meeting a plan for permanent organization. (Dr. Granville, Jacobs and Manhart were appointed).

—Representatives of boards of trustees and boards of education invited.

That it is the sense of this Conference that representation on the part of our several boards of trustees and boards of education is especially desired at all future conferences.

1912—Officers asked to prepare a Constitution

That the officers be instructed to arrange another conference, similar to this, during the year 1913 and be instructed to prepare a constitution.

1916—New constitution again referred to officers

That the construction of a constitution and framing of by-laws be referred to the new officers.

1926—Regarding increase in membership—from Report of the Treasurer.

In order to increase the number of our individual members, I desire to recommend to the Conference, that the present custom by which teachers in institutions which are members of the Conference, have individual membership privileges by virtue of that membership, be changed. We can undoubtedly add at least 100 new individual members if we have it understood that institutional dues do not admit individual members of faculties to membership.

There are still many Lutheran institutions which are not members of the Conference. Would it not be well to appoint a Special Committe or a Membership Secretary, to carry on an active propaganda for new members, both institutional and individual?

1929—Continuance of the Seminary men in the NLEC

That this Conference recommend the continuance of the Seminary men in the meetings of the National Lutheran Educational Conference, both because of the unique opportunity afforded for consideration of their own peculiar problems and because this is an integral part of the work of the church.

—*Unity of College and Seminary interests.*

That it is the sense of the Conference that Seminary and College interests are identical; that the group is a unity and that as such we shall go forward in promoting the educational work of our great Lutheran church.

1929—Invitation to Canadian Lutheran Schools.

That we invite Canadian Lutheran Schools to participate in our next meeting.

1929—To meet the same week as the Association of American Colleges

That we meet Tuesday and Wednesday of the week in which the Association of American Colleges holds its convention.

1930—Time and place of meeting

That the National Lutheran Educational Conference hereafter meet at the same time and place with the Association of American Colleges.

1937—Proposed Eastern regional conference.

That the Executive Committee be requested to consider the possibility and advisability of sponsoring an Eastern Regional Conference of Lutheran College faculty members, similar to those held at St. Olaf College in 1935 and at Augustana College in 1936.

1942—Regarding membership of deaconess training schools.

That the deaconess training schools be denied admission to the NLEC as institutional members, but that the trainees and faculty members be welcomed to join as individual members.

1942—Proposal for a National Lutheran College Commission.

That the Executive Committee give careful consideration to the advisability of organizing a National Lutheran College Commission of the NLEC whose chief function shall be to represent Lutheran educational interests in relation to government agencies, The American Association Colleges, and The National Conference of Church Related Colleges.

1947—Membership of Valparaiso University

That the application for membership of Valparaiso University, submitted by O. P. Kretzmann, be approved.

1947—Office of Historian and Statistician

That a permanent office of Conference historian and statistician be created and a qualified person be elected upon recommendation of the nominating committee. (Dr. Mildred E. Winston was appointed to this office.)

1947—Regarding representation in the Conference of teachers from non-Lutheran Institutions.

1. That the National Lutheran Educational Conference request the student Commission of the National Lutheran Council to make a survey of Lutheran teachers in non-Lutheran institutions and present such a list to the Executive Committee of the NLEC.

2. That the Executive Committee of the NLEC take steps to provide representation of these teachers in the NLEC on such basis as the Executive Committee may determine.

1955—Admission of Executive heads of deaconess training schools to membership.

That the executive heads of the Baltimore Training School for deaconesses and the Philadelphia Training School for deaconesses be admitted to membership in the NLEC with the annual fee of $10.00.

1955—Regarding Commission on Research.

The commission on research as such seems to have been abolished, but in the new "rules of procedure" it was provided "that there shall be a commission on records and research, consisting of the chief executive of each member board of education."

1962—Membership of the Board of Trustees

That the National Lutheran Educational Conference be asked to revise Article V of the Constitution at the next meeting as follows:

a—That the words, "Board of Trustees and its Powers" be substituted for the words, "Executive Committee and its Powers".

b—That the Board of Trustees be constituted each year with four representatives of colleges: presidents/faculty; two representatives of seminaries: presidents/faculty; and one representative of a church board: seminary/college.

c—That the president and vice-president of the Conference shall be included among the representatives of their particular groups.

d—That the retiring president shall be a member of the Board of Trustees, and be included as a representative of his particular group.

e—That the president of the Conference shall be the chairman of the Board of Trustees.

f—That the Executive Director shall be an advisory member of the Board of Trustees.

g—That the words, "Executive Committee", be deleted wherever found in this Article.

1964—Regarding proposed new inter-Lutheran Agency

That the NLEC indicates its approval of the proposal to provide a related but autonomous place for the NLEC in a new inter-Lutheran Agency.

That the officers of the NLEC be authorized to represent the NLEC in any consultation and negotiation as to the details of relationship to the proposed inter-Lutheran Agency.

1966—Regarding LCUSA

That, since communications have been received from officials of Lutheran Church bodies asking that the possible relationship of the NLEC to LCUSA be reconsidered, a special Committee of the NLEC be authorized to confer with the proper committee of LCUSA regarding such possible relationship, and that the said special Committee be composed of *Gould Wickey, Paul Dieckman, Erling Jensen,* and *A. O. Fuerbringer.*

It was unanimously approved, after including the name of *Charles Balcer* in the Committee, in order to include a representative from the institutions of the American Lutheran Church.

That this special Committee of the NLEC be directed to communicate the results of its findings to the Executive Committee, who in turn shall report its recommendations to the NLEC at the next annual meeting, regularly held in January or at a specially called meeting which may be considered the annual meeting.

1966—Regarding number of sessions

That the sessions of future annual meetings of the NLEC be reduced from five to three, to be held Sunday afternoon and evening and Monday morning, or at such time as may fit best with the programs of other educational agencies which have meetings during the same period.

13—Other Organizations

1921—To the Council of Church Boards of Education

That we ask our representatives to the Council of Church Boards of Education to see what can be done to defend our church colleges against the modern vocational trend with respect to entrance requirements.

1928—To the Association of American Colleges

That we address the Association of American Colleges to make the subject of better College Training a matter of serious study with a view of making some definite recommendations along this line in the near future to the Graduate Schools of our country.

1931—Regarding the Liberal Arts College Movement

That, in view of the aims of the Liberal Arts College Movement as now made clear, we give approval to it, and suggest that membership therein be considered by each of our Lutheran colleges.

1932—The Liberal Arts College Movement

That this Association express its firm faith in the Liberal Arts College as an important and indispensable factor in the educational field. The Church dare not omit or fail to emphasize the value of the Liberal Arts College for the training of Church leadership.

1932—Expansion of NLEC so as to include workers in elementary and secondary Christian education

In answer to the question raised by our Secretary whether it would be for the best interests of this Conference that the Conference be expanded so as to include workers and those interested in elementary and secondary Christian education, your Committee is of the opinion, that, although fully cognizant of the importance of the primary and secondary levels of the educational work of the Church, it would *not* be wise to include this aspect of the work within the scope of the conference, chiefly because of time limitation and the desire to concentrate on the fields now represented.

1932—Opposition to U.S. Department of Education

That this Conference does not look with favor upon the suggestion that a Department of Education with a secretary of education at its head be established in the federal government. We believe, with the report of the National Advisory Committee on Education, that the emphasis should be placed on local autonomy and responsibility and away from the strong tendency towards centralization in the national capital.

1932—Cooperation with News Bulletin of the National Lutheran Council

We commend as valuable and desirable, a Lutheran Educational News Bulletin. We recommend that a working agreement with the News Bulletin of the National Lutheran Council be sought, whereby the cooperation of as many as possible of our educational institutions may be listed and the Bulletin be given a proportionately wide distribution. We recommend that the officers of the Association be granted power to act in the matter.

1934—Regarding the Liberal Arts College Movement

Having noted with interest the action of the Liberal Arts College Movement and the College Department of the Council of Church Boards of Education in merging their work, we express the earnest hope that the new enterprise thus inaugurated may result in an emphasis upon the distinctively religious features of the work of the Church-related Colleges, and a more effective promotion of the common interests of these Institutions.

1939—Regarding the inclusion of faculty members in Social Security

1. That the National Lutheran Educational Conference in Convention assembled on January 10, 1939, endorses the recommendation contained in the final report of the Advisory Council of the Federal Social Security

Board, providing for inclusion in the Social Security Act of faculty members of church related colleges, academies and theological seminaries.

2. That copies of this resolution be sent to the Federal Social Security Board and to the secretary of the Association of American Colleges and Universities.

1947—Regarding a Division of Higher Education in the National Lutheran Council

That the Executive Committee of the NLEC be directed to study the need and desirability of recommending to the National Lutheran Council the creation of a Division of Higher Education within the National Lutheran Council and that the National Lutheran Council be apprised of this action.

1947—To the American Section, Lutheran World Federation, regarding exchange scholarships.

That the NLEC respectfully requests the American Section of the Lutheran World Federation to give favorable consideration to the establishment of undergraduate as well as graduate exchange scholarships with foreign countries.

—Thanks to National Lutheran Council

That the NLEC is grateful to the National Lutheran Council for the grant of $70,000 from the funds of the Service Commission, to be used in providing more adequate spiritual service to veterans in our respective Lutheran Colleges. Since the grant is for a two-year period, and the need will continue for at least four years, we respectfully request that the National Lutheran Council make provision for a similar grant two years hence.

1953—Regarding Korean G.I. Bill

Whereas the Veterans Readjustment Assistance Act of 1952 (P.L. 550) involves factors prejudicial to non-tax-supported colleges and universities not found in previous GI legislation; therefore, be it resolved,

That the NLEC respectfully urge the Congress of the United States of America to revise the Veterans Readjustment Assistance Act of 1952 so as provide for the separation of tuition allowance and subsistence allowance.

1957—Encouragement to Boards of Higher Education to make larger funds available for obtaining qualified teachers.

Whereas, there is a clearly recognized continuing and growing need for qualified and committed teachers in our Lutheran colleges; and

Whereas, every laudable effort should be made to increase the supply as expeditiously as possible; therefore, be it resolved

That the following specific technique be used without undue delays

a) That the faculties in our various colleges be urged to set up committees specifically charged with the responsibility of discovering and encouraging talented undergraduates to prepare themselves for teaching in our Lutheran colleges;

b) That the NLEC encourage the Boards of Higher Education of the respective Lutheran church bodies to invest larger sums of money in the educating of Lutheran men and women for positions on the faculties of both seminaries and colleges.

c) That, as soon as possible, the Placement Bureau expand its services by establishing a department for the pooling of information about prospective college and seminary teachers, it being understood that the necessary financial support would have to be equitably shared.

1957—To the Division of Colleges and University Work, NLC, regarding students from foreign lands.

That the Executive Committee be asked to consult with the Division of Colleges and University Work of the National Lutheran Council concerning the possibility of giving greater emphasis and more concentrated direction to the sharing of hospitality to students in America from foreign lands.

14 —Placement Bureau, Teachers' Directory

1916—Central Bureau for Teachers

It was moved by J. A. Morehead, president of Roanoke College, "that a Committee of three be chosen to arrange for a central bureau of teachers to list teachers eligible for Lutheran college positions and submit the list to college presidents."

(President Vigness appointed: Rev. H. R. Gold, President J. A. W. Haas, and Mr. W. C. Stoever)

1923—Request of Lutheran Bureau, NLC.

That the Lutheran Bureau of the National Lutheran Counci be requested to open a Teachers' Bureau, in order to assist Lutheran Educational Institutions in finding capable professors and instructors when they are needed.

1931—Teachers' Directory discontinued.

That the publication of the Lutheran Teachers' Directory be not continued at this time, and that, in order to serve the purpose originally intended, the Secretary be requested to secure and transmit to all Lutheran colleges information regarding Lutheran teachers available for positions. It is suggested that information regarding each such prospective teacher be mimeographed on a single sheet and forwarded to our schools promptly for information and filing.

1947—To establish Lutheran Teachers' Placement Bureau.

That there be established by the National Lutheran Educational Conference, in conjunction with the Student Service Commission of the National Lutheran Council, a Lutheran Teachers' Placement Bureau, and that the Executive Committee of the NLEC be authorized to expend up to $1,000 annually for this work.

15. Prizes, Scholarships, Fellowships

1910—To establish one or more fellowships.

That we recommend the establishment of one or more fellowships for the training of teachers in connection with our Lutheran schools.

1931—To establish an Annual Prize Essay Contest.

A typed resolution is in the archives which proposes an annual prize essay contest "open to any student enrolled in any Lutheran college or theological seminary in the United States or Canada". This contest was to begin in 1932, and was to have three prizes: 1st, $50; 2nd, $35; and 3rd, $15. The first prize essay was to be read at the following annual convention of the Conference and published in the proceedings. It appears that the subject on which the essays were to be written was to be selected from year to year.

There are no minutes available, which would indicate whether this resolution was ever adopted or effected.

16. Public Relations: Promotion, Publicity

1923—Urge for greater publicity

That the Secretary of the Conference, in order to secure greater publicity for this Association, be instructed to send out announcements of the next meeting to all Lutheran official publications.

1925—Approval of Martin Luther Film

That we convey to the Lutheran Film Division of New York City our sincere appreciation for the showing of the Martin Luther Film. In view of the recognized fact that one of the most effective means of impressing historical events upon the minds of people is by visual instruction in a true and impressive manner, we heartily recommend this film to the institutions which we represent and to all our churches who may desire to provide for their people profitable and instructive entertainment.

1926—Proper publicity to be developed

That we consider proper publicity for our Church, for our colleges and other institutions an important matter, to be cultivated and developed and that we express our appreciation to the National Lutheran Council for the service it is rendering our Church through the Public Bureau.

That the officers, in consultation with Mr. Elson, devise a plan for national publicity on behalf of Lutheran colleges, to be conducted through the Publicity Bureau of the National Lutheran Council, and that the plan be put into operation as soon as may prove practicable.

1926—Greater publicity through friendly visitors

It was voted, (1) to ask all general Lutheran bodies in this country to appoint friendly visitors to our meetings, the conferences retaining the same informal character as heretofore, and (2) that through these visitors, the

Secretary endeavor to secure a reference to the work of the National Lutheran Educational Conference in the printed minutes of the various bodies.

1927—Handbook of Information

It was voted to approve a plan for the publication of a handbook setting forth the aims and purposes of the organization to be used in soliciting individual memberships and for other general publicity purposes. The officers were requested to prepare and publish this bulletin.

1931—Christian Education Sunday

That, whenever possible, the Sunday before the meeting of the Conference be designated Christian Education Sunday and that all Lutheran Church bodies having congregations in the city of meeting endeavor to have speakers in their respective churches (congregations).

—Academic Occasions

That we note with pleasure the increasing emphasis being placed upon academic occasions, such as inaugurations of Presidents, installations of professors and dedications of buildings in our colleges and seminaries; and we commend to all our schools the practice of observing these occasions in a formal way, and of sending invitations to the educational institutions of the country.

1935—Joint publicity for institutions

That the Conference believes that the joint publicity or simultaneous publicity for our institutions of higher learning whenever possible, is desirable and valuable. It would suggest to those who have charge of the general educational publicity within the various synodical groups, to make every effort to collaborate and coordinate their efforts in this field.

1938—Regarding exhibits

That a director of exhibits be appointed to take charge of the annual convention exhibits, and that he be allowed traveling expenses, meals, hotel, also some clerical assistance if necessary.

a. That the secretary be instructed to write a letter to all member colleges calling attention to the enlargement of the exhibits to include monographs, books, and other contributions by faculty members.

b. That the Lutheran Publishing Houses be invited to participate with their exhibits.

1944—Improving relations of schools with constituencies

That the Executive Committee request W. Emerson Reck, Public Relations Director of Colgate University, to prepare suggestions for improving the relations of our Lutheran colleges to their constituency and that these suggestions be presented to this Conference at the next annual convention.

1953—Cooperation in Promotion

That the NLEC encourage the various boards of education or committees to prepare and put into effect a coordinated program of promotion among our Lutheran people, utilizing particularly the month of April and Christian College Day as an occasion when alumni and others may be more effectively solicited for funds.

1959—A single bulletin or journal for Lutheran facilities

The Executive Director reported that he was authorized to discuss with officials of the Association of Lutheran Faculties and the Division of College and University Work, NLC, the problem of the possibility of a single journal or bulletin for the Lutheran faculties.

(On the basis of preliminary inquiries, it did not seem feasible.)

1960—Publicity Folder

The Executive Director reported that he had prepared a publicity folder entitled, "Why You Should Support a Quality Education", with a printing of 15,000 at a total cost of $265.90. Three thousand were sold to a Board of Education for $45.00. The folder was used by the Conference to obtain more funds for the Fellowship Program.

1962—Committee on Film to Promote Lutheran Colleges

To a meeting of the Board of Directors on March 29, 1962, the Executive Director reported on his conferences with individuals in Minneapolis regarding the composition of a desirable committee to work on a film for the promotion of our Lutheran colleges. The Committee was composed of: O. W. Toelke, Robert Mortvedt, W. Emerson Reck, Henry Endress, and Norman Fintel, with R. H. Gerberding and Gould Wickey as Advisors.

(This committee had several meetings, scripts were written by competent writers, but apparently no script was found satisfactory. The Lutheran Brotherhood Insurance paid the expenses of the Committee and the fees for the script writing.)

17. Seminaries, Theological

1910—A Fourth Year at Theological Seminaries

That a fourth year be added to the courses of our Theological Seminaries this added year to afford opportunities for students to do specializing work, the successful completion of which shall be rewarded with the degree of Bachelor of Divinity.

1919—Council of Theological Seminaries

The Council of Theological Seminaries held its first meeting at the Chicago Lutheran Theological Seminary, Maywood, Illinois July 26-30, 1919.

1926—Relation of seminaries to the Conference

It was voted, (1) that all theological seminaries be urged to hold active membership in this Association, (2) that on the program of the Association each year one or two papers be presented on such subjects as are of interest to college and seminary faculties; also, (3) that representatives of seminaries in attendance at the annual meeting hold a conference of their own to discuss such subjects as are of special interest in seminary work.

1933—A Summer Theological Institute

That the conference hereby calls special attention to the suggestion of a summer theological institute made by Dr. Bergendoff, and that we recommend the appointment of a committee with power to put on such an institute during the coming summer to try out the proposition, and on the basis of such an experiment report back to this conference at its next convention.

1964—A Consultation on Theological Education

That the National Lutheran Educational Conference express its appreciation to the National Lutheran Council, Department of Theological Cooperation, for Pastor Westlund's presentation with reference to the desirability for a study of theological education.

That this meeting of the National Lutheran Educational Conference endorse the proposal for an all-Lutheran consultation on theological education.

That the National Lutheran Educational Conference request the Department of Theological Cooperation to take appropriate steps to send a letter to the participating bodies of the National Lutheran Council and the Lutheran Church-Missouri Synod requesting the appointment of three representatives from each body to initiate plans for a consultation on theological education.

18. Students . . . Campus Ministry

1923—Ministry to Students commended

That we heartily commend the work of following up our Lutheran students in the various state institutions as it is now being conducted.

1925—Student pastors urged to bring the ministration of the church to the students

Recognizing the tremendous importance of all the influences under which our young people live during the years of their college life and also fully aware of the indisputable fact that those influences, especially in large tax-supported universities throughout the land, tend to undermine and to shake the simple faith in revealed truth, we heartily commend all efforts of our student pastors which would bring the ministration of our Church to the students in such schools.

1927—Interest of students commended.

That the National Lutheran Educational Conference notes with pleasure the increased interest on the part of the Lutheran students in denominational colleges and undenominational institutions in the problems as well as the opportunities of the Lutheran Church.

1958—Federal aid to students

It is recognized that our country and the world face a future in which the need for higher education will be such as to call for the largest possible measure of support from all sources and the most thoughtful and efficient use of all resources that become available, and it is further recognized that the critical importance of higher education to our national welfare is likely to put the resources of the Federal Government behind the program of higher education in ways and to degrees only partly determined at this time.

We, therefore, urge the following considerations upon all who will share in deciding the pattern and extent of such support:

1) It is to the best interest of all education that any program of Federal support permit and encourage the full and free operation and development of the dual system of education, public and private, as it has developed in our country.

2) The support of education by grants to individual students permits a broader support of American higher education than is the case when such support consists of subsidies to institutions.

3) Since the need for trained leadership is diverse and is often most serious where least apparent, the greatest contribution to the national welfare will be financial assistance to students on a broad basis, giving priority to individual qualifications and personal need rather than to vocational objectives and interests.

J. N. Brown

President, Concordia College
Moorhead, Minn.
NLEC
Vice-President, 1928
President, 1929

E. F. Pihlblad

President, Bethany College
Lindsborg, Kansas
NLEC
Vice-President, 1920, 1927
President, 1928

97

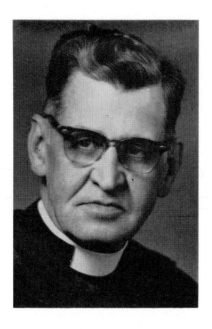

Karl E. Mattson

President, Augustana
  Theological Seminary
  Rock Island, Ill.
NLEC
  Vice-President, 1962
  President, 1963

Voight R. Cromer

President, Lenoir-Rhyne College
  Hickory, N. C.
NLEC
  Vice-President, 1954
  President, 1955

98

C. As seen in the Research Projects, Studies and Surveys

A list of the research projects, studies and surveys, arranged chronologically according to the year when made or presented to the Conference, is given in Chapter III, where the special significance of some of them will be noted.

During the first decade, 1910-1920, no significant study is recorded. However, in the 1920 proceedings is printed an exhibit of the schools related to the various Lutheran Church bodies with interesting statistics for each school.

From 1920 to 1930 much interest seemed to have been manifested in the Bible knowledge of college students and in the Bible courses which should be given at Lutheran colleges and seminaries.

From 1933 to 1940 attention seemed to turn from the curriculum to the student. Here are found papers on the motives of students in attending Lutheran colleges, the attitudes of Lutheran college students, problems of personal work in Lutheran colleges, factors affecting the scholarship of college students, job analysis of personnel functions in Lutheran colleges, and freshman orientation in Lutheran colleges.

Beginning in 1937 and continuing for thirty years, almost annually, some report was made concerning enrollments in Lutheran colleges and seminaries.

Although the financing of Lutheran colleges was referred to occasionally in the early years 1910 to 1940, it was in 1947 that surveys began to be made of finances in Lutheran colleges, surveys as to income, budgets, and building fund appeals, etc.

In 1950 attention was given to faculty studies and research, and a review of the productivity of Lutheran college faculties during the previous decade. Faculty women in Lutheran colleges was presented in 1951.

Persons whose names are the most frequently related to studies are: H. J. Arnold, Erland Nelson, Paul Heisey, M. J. Neuberg, Emory Lindquist, Mildred Winston, William L. Young and Gould Wickey.

Wm. L. Young, Ph.D.

Executive Secretary,
Board of Education, former,
American Lutheran Church
NLEC
Vice-President, 1932
President, 1933

Erland Nelson, Ph.D.

President, Dana College, and later
Carthage College
NLEC
President, 1934

O. J. Johnson

President, Gustavus Adolphus College, St. Peter, Minn.
NLEC
Vice-President, 1925
President, 1931

Emory Lindquist, Ph. D.

President, Bethany College, Lindsborg, Kansas
NLEC
Vice-President, 1946
President, 1947

D. As Seen in special Events and Programs

Speakers at Dinner Sessions

Beginning in the 1930s and continuing through the years, the programs of the annual meetings indicate an effort to obtain special speakers for an evening dinner session, to which Lutherans from the local churches were invited. The speakers and their subjects will show the wide range of interest.

1924 Rev. G. U. Wenner, D.D., New York City, called the pioneer in the modern Religious Education Movement in America.

1930 Rev. F. H. Knubel, D.D., President, United Lutheran Church in America, "Our Lutheran Heritage and its Challenge."

1932 Honorable John F. Kramer, Commissioner, Volstead Act, 1921-22. "Knowledge is Power, But . . ."

1933 Honorable John M. Nelson, Congressman from Wisconsin, "As a Layman Sees It."

1934 Rev. G. A. Brandelle, D.D., President, Augustana Synod, "Christian Higher Education: its Meaning, Its Purpose, Its Means."

1936 Dr. John Finley, an editor of the New York Times, "My Times."

1937 Baron von Tippelskirch, Consul General of the German Reich, Boston, Mass.

1945 Rev. W. H. Traub, D.D., Pastor, Kountze Memorial Lutheran Church, Omaha, Neb.

1946 Rev. Ralph H. Long, D.D., Executive Director, National Lutheran Council

1947 Dr. Dwayne Orton, Director of Education, International Business Machines Corp., "Education to Match these Times."

1952 Honorable Edward J. Thye, United States Senator from Minnesota
Professor Harold Grimm, Ph.D., Ohio State University, "Christian Higher Education and the Conscience of our Time."

1953 President Charles B. Foelsch, Ph.D. Pacific Lutheran Theological Seminary, "The Road Ahead."

1955 Professor H. Richard Niebuhr, Ph.D., Yale University "The Theological Foundation for Lutheran Higher Education."
Rev. Oscar A. Benson, D.D., President Augustana Ev. Lutheran Church, "What the Church Expects of its Colleges."

1960 Professor Roland Bainton, Ph.D., Yale University Divinity School, "Luther and Education." Fiftieth Anniversary of the Conference.

1961 Rev. Martin Marty, D.D., Associate Editor, The Christian Century, "The Liberal Arts and the Christian Faith."

1962 Blair Stewart, Executive Director, Associated Colleges of the Mid-West, "Cooperation and the Future of American Liberal Arts Colleges."

1964 Professor Jaroslav J. Pelikan, Jr., Ph.D., Professor, Yale University

Divinity School, "Creative Tensions: Catholicism and Protestantism."

1965 H. T. Morse, Ph.D., Dean, General College, University of Minnesota, "Educational Integrity."

1966 Edward A. Lindell, Ed.D., Dean, College of Liberal Arts and Sciences, University of Denver, "Campus Rebellions."

1967 Dialogue on Authority and Inquiry

Rev. Albert J. Zabala, S.J., Chairman, Department of Theology, University of San Francisco, "Christian Authority."

Rev. Warren A. Quanbeck, Ph.D., Professor, Department of Systematic Theology, Luther Seminary, St. Paul. "The Lutheran Understanding of Authority."

Lutheran Education Sunday and Sunday Evening Mass Meetings

Beginning also in the 1930s was the effort to get representatives of the colleges and seminaries as speakers in the various Lutheran churches on the Sunday when the annual meeting was held in any city. Sometimes every Lutheran church in the convention city had a speaker as guest preacher, or as speaker at the Sunday School hour. One hindrance to this plan was the fact that often the churches had communion services on the second Sunday in January, which frequently was the Sunday when the Conference would hold its meeting.

Later in the 1930s and continuing into the 1940s was the attempt to have a Sunday Evening Mass meeting in which all Lutheran churches would join. Whether this was possible was dependent upon the custom in that community of Sunday evening services. It appeared to be more successful when other church groups related to the Council of Church Boards of Education would join in such a Sunday evening mass meeting. This plan also was changed, since many denominations wanted to have their own educational meetings Sunday evening.

Conferences on Evangelism

At Minneapolis during January 23-27, 1952 the National Lutheran Council held a Conference on Evangelism. For that event the NLEC had prepared an elaborate display with a map of North America showing the location of Lutheran colleges and seminaries under the caption, "*Your Colleges and Seminaries Are Sharing Christ Today!*" Although the Conference approved the project, apparently it did not have sufficient funds to pay for the project. The Board of Christian Education of the Evangelical Lutheran Church, at the suggestion of Dr. Sidney Rand, then the executive secretary of that Board, agreed to pay the balance. This evoked much appreciation on the part of the members of the Conference. But the records show that a display was approved by an Evangelism Conference to be held in Milwaukee in 1955, and that the NLEC paid $225 on Nov. 22, 1955 for that display.

Incorporation and Location of Offices in Washington

One of the most important events in the history of the NLEC was the decision at the 1958 annual meeting in Miami to locate its national office in Washington and to incorporate. Incorporation was important since that encouraged some significant financial gifts towards the Martin Luther Fellowship Program. Location of a national office in Washington was the recognition of Washington as an outstanding educational center, especially in light of the growing pace which the Government was taking in making grants to educational institutions for housing, facilities, and research. This location was also important, since most of the national educational organizations have their headquarters in Washington. Since 1958 the executive director was able to render valuable service to the colleges in contacting officials of the U.S. Office of Education as well as the offices of many national educational organizations. In turn, very frequent inquiries and requests from these organizations to the office of the NLEC were promptly answered. The executive director was invited to attend committee and other group meetings under the auspices of the U.S. Office of Education, to which he would not have been invited had the office been located outside Washington. The same is true in relations with the American Council on Education.

Silver Anniversary Convention of the Conference

With Dr. H. J. Arnold as secretary, an elaborate progarm was prepared to celebrate the twenty-fifth anniversary of the Conference in Chicago. Besides an Informal Reception and Tea tendered by President Walter Dill Scott and the Faculty of Northwestern University in Thorne Hall on the Chicago Campus of the University, and an Informal Reception tendered by President L. Franklin Gruber and the Faculty of the Chicago Lutheran Theological Seminary at Maywood, and a banquet session with all living past presidents of the Conference as guests and speakers, arrangements were made for a Sunday evening meeting in the Stevens Hotel with Lutherans from the city invited. The presiding officer was Mr. Theodore A. Dahlstrom, President, Regional Federation of Lutheran Brotherhoods. The principal feature was a symposium on "Whither the Lutheran Church." The speakers and their subjects were President L. W. Boe, St. Olaf College, "The International Outlook,"; Rev. Peter Peterson, President, Illinois Conference of the Augustana Synod, "Missions"; Rev. E. J. Braulick, President, Wartburg College, "Social Service"; Mr. Joseph G. Norby, Superintendent, Columbia Hospital, Milwaukee, "Cooperation"; and Dr. Gould Wickey, Executive secretary, Board of Education, ULCA., "Education." Dr. H. J. Arnold, Director, Division of Special Schools, Wittenberg College was the leader during the discussion period.

Memorial Column at the New York World's Fair

At a cost of $1,500 the Conference agreed to pay for a memorial column to honor a Lutheran pioneer in the Court of Christian Pioneers, Protestant and Orthodox Center, at the New York World's Fair. The

Conference's column honored Philip Melanchthon and was dedicated July 19, 1964. The other Lutheran pioneers honored were: Martin Luther, J. S. Bach, H. M. Muhlenberg, C. F. W. Walther, William A. Passavant, F. Melius Christiansen, and Dag Hammarskjöld. President A. O. Fuerbringer, Concordia Seminary, St. Louis represented the Conference at the dedication.

The bronze plaque attached to the Conference's column reads

Philip Melanchthon, 1497-1560, internationally famous scholar, teacher and churchman, friend and helper of Luther, author of Augsburg Confession and other definitive works.

These memorial columns were supposed to go to the owners, but because of labor conditions and requirements it was found too expensive to remove the pylons. In fact, one institution which was ready to move its men on the Fair Grounds to remove several pylons reported, "We were not permitted to move our own men into the Fair Grounds because of New York City Union regulations which must be the most demanding in the world. The cost proposed to us by the demolition contractors for the removal of the pylons to our campus was so exorbitant that made it impossible for us to follow through." Susquehanna University had intended to use several pylons around a traffic circle, but since that was impossible, they did obtain some of the plaques which will be appropriately placed for student and public observation. It is likely that the Conference will never be misled into such a project again, although there is appreciation for the opportunity of honoring the "friend and helper of Luther" and the author of the Augsburg Confession.

Celebration of the 450th Anniversary of the Reformation

Mention has already been made above (in the section on Speakers at Dinner Sessions) about the Dialogue on Authority and Inquiry held at the annual meeting in January 1967. This was probably the first major event in the United States during 1967 in recognition of the 450th anniversary of the Reformation. With a Catholic and a Lutheran theologian participating in the dialogue, the event was the more significant.

This is not the first time that a Catholic educator appeared on the program of the Conference. At Cleveland in 1962 with the general theme "Current Influences Related to Lutheran Higher Education," and the subtheme, "Church-State Relations in Education", Monsignor F. G. Hochwalt, Ph.D., Director, Department of Education, National Catholic Welfare Conference, Washington, D.C., and Albert G. Huegli, Ph.D., Vice-President for Academic Affairs, Valparaiso University, Valparaiso, Indiana, made stimulating presentations. During the discussion period, Monsignor Hochwalt declared he agreed about 95% with Dr. Huegli.

During 1966 the Office of the Conference acted as the liaison between the Coordinator's Office of the 450th Reformation Anniversary and

Lutheran colleges and seminaries. With the theme, LIFE-NEW LIFE, the General Anniversary Committee planned to stimulate interest and active response in the celebration by contacting not only all parishes but also all Lutheran organizations and Lutheran educational institutions. The Rev. Dale E. Griffin, as Coordinator, worked closely with the Executive Director of the NLEC. The presidents of the Lutheran colleges and seminaries in Canada and the United States appointed at each school a faculty member or a special committee to function as coordinator of the various types of programs on the campus. The NLEC office gathered various suggestions of possible programs for colleges and seminaries, and mailed them to each school. In addition, from the schools were received the names of more than 100 faculty members who would be willing to speak at various congregational and community events. This list of speakers with their institutions and subjects of their addresses were mailed to the colleges and seminaries, and also 500 copies were sent to the Coordinator for distribution to the chairmen of the area committees. In addition, to the colleges and seminaries were mailed these items: Manual for Area Anniversary Committees, Guide to Reformation Literature, and Daily Bible Reading Plan.

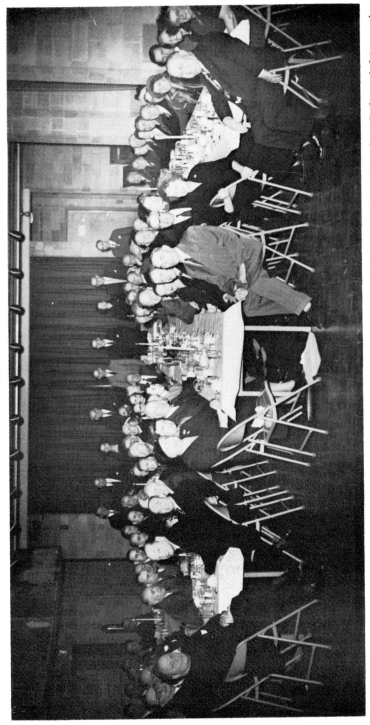

Some of the Lutheran Educators and Leaders who heard Senator Thye of Minnesota (standing fourth from left) speak to the dinner session of the National Lutheran Educational Conference gathered in the Parish Hall of Luther Place Memorial Church, Washington, D.C., January 1952.

The Rev. Charles B. Foelsch, Ph.D., president, Pacific Lutheran Theological Seminary, Berkeley, Cal., delivers the address at the dinner session of the NLEC during the annual meeting held at Los Angeles in 1953. The sessions were held in Angelica Lutheran Church and Dr. Foelsch spoke on "The Road Ahead."

The Display of the NLEC at the National Lutheran Council Evangelism Conference held at Minneapolis on January 23-27, 1952.

The Rev. Dr. Alfred O. Fuebringer, president of Concordia Theological Seminary, St. Louis, representing the National Lutheran Educational Conference, places floral piece before the memorial column honoring Philip Melanchthon in the Court of Christian Pioneers, Protestant and Orthodox Center, New York World's Fair. This column and seven others were dedicated to Lutheran pioneers at noon on Lutheran Day at the Fair, July 19, 1964. Other Lutheran pioneers honored were: Martin Luther, J. S. Bach, H. M. Muhlenberg, C. F. W. Walther, William A. Passavant, F. Melius Christensen, and Dag Hammerskjöld. Miss Mae Lee and Mr. Robert Soohoo, of True Light Lutheran Church, New York City, assist with the dedication. —NLC News Photo Service

A partial view of those attending the dinner session of the NLEC during the 53rd Annual Convention at Los Angeles, Cal., January 15-16, 1967. This marks the 57th year of the NLEC.

Leaders at the dinner session of the annual meeting of the NLEC held in Los Angeles, Cal., January 15-16, 1967. Pictured are, left to right, Dr. Robert Mortvedt, president, Pacific Lutheran University and president, NLEC; the Rev. Albert J. Zabala, S.J., Chairman, Department of Theology, University of San Francisco, and the Rev. Warren A. Quanbeck, Ph.D., professmor of Systematic Theology, Luther Seminary, St. Paul. The latter two had a dialogue on "Authority and Inquiry", which was presented in recognition of the 450th Anniversary of the Protestant Reformation. Their papers were published in the 1967 proceedings of the NLEC.

E. Appendix to Chapter II.

Alphabetical list of Authors and Speakers together with the Titles of the Papers read and the Years when presented at the Annual Meetings of the National Lutheran Educational Conference.

The list which follows was gathered from the official minutes, the printed programs, and the printed proceedings of the annual meetings, so far as they were available. Sometimes papers read were not available for printing in the proceedings. The following list generally omits reports of commissions and certain studies, since most of the significant studies and surveys are noted in Chapter III under the title of Research Projects and Studies. This list provides interesting information as to the persons who participated in the programs of the Conference, the subjects which they discussed, and the years when the subjects were discussed. This will indicate how relevant the programs of the Conference were to the varied conditions and circumstances of the different decades of this twentieth century. The letters (RT) mean Round Table.

A

Aasgaard, J. A.
—College Finances 1922
Aberly, John
—The Spiritual Growth of Students in our Seminaries 1929
—The Seminary Library 1931
Ackerman, Carl
—The Bible as Literature or the Bible in Literature, Which? 1926
Aikens, C. T.
—Religious Care of Students in Lutheran Institutions 1910
Alschwede, Arthur
—The Church and the Government of its Educational Institution:
as an Executive of a Board of Theological Education Sees It 1965
Anderson, George
—The Christian Teacher as seen by the State University 1959
Anderson, L. A.
—Work for Lutheran Students at State University 1919
Anderson, Oscar A.
—Devotional Meditations 1964
Andreen, G.
—Financing a Church College 1912
—What should be the Attitude of our Lutheran Colleges toward
movement to abolish Latin as Requisite for the AB Degree? 1918
—What is the Relative Importance of the Service rendered by
the Christian College—1, in training men for the Ministry;

124

I

Ingvolstad, O.

J

Jacobs, Charles M.

K

Kastner, E. W.

132

Q

R

S

Sawvel, Franklin B.
—The Present Status of Lutheran Educational Work in America   1910
Schaaf, Laurence J.
—Tools and Techniques for Carrying out the Personnel Services   1939
—Status of Personnel Counseling in 3 types of Institutions
    of Higher Learning   1941
Schaefer, Henry
—The Teaching of Hebrew in conformity with modern Language
    Methods   1922
—Post-Graduate Work for Lutheran Ministers in America   1928
Schaeffer, H. Brent
—Financial Support of our Church Schools   1928
Scherer, James
—Education for Missionaries   1961
Schiotz, Fredrik
—A Division of Christian Education in the National
    Lutheran Council   1961
Schnabel, Robert
—Education for the Ministry   1961
Schulz, Rudolph G., Jr.
—The Challenge of the new Social Order to the Church-Related
    College   1939
Schneider, J. P.
—The Social Life of the Church College   1912
Schroder, Martin
—The Ministry to the Disposed in rural Communities   1940
Schuh, L. H.
—How Obtain our own Students who belong to us   1910
Seagle, Inez
—Social Implications of Campus Rebellions   1966
Sears, Donald
—America as the Land of the Lost Present   1960
Sebelius, S. J.
—Some Moral and Religious Aspects of European University
    Life   1925
Seegers, J. Conrad
—The Influence of Statism upon the Administrative Policies of
    Lutheran Colleges   1954
Segerhammar, Carl W.
—Lutheran Higher Education for California   1953
Serenius, C. A.
—Problems of Personnel Work in Lutheran Colleges:
    Personnel Services   1939
—More Effective Methods of Promotion and Publicity   1940

Steimle, A.
—A Suggestion for our Colleges 1933
Stewart, Blair
—Cooperation and the Future of American Liberal Arts Colleges 1962
Stoughton, C. C.
—The Christian College,—Bulwark of American Democracy 1939
—The One Course Plan 1944
—The Church, the College, and the Gospel 1958
—Financial Subsidy for Seminaries from Business and Industry 1959
—New Dimensions in the small University 1960
—Program of Lay Training at Wittenberg University, its Genesis 1962
Stoughton, Donald
—Program of Lay Training at Wittenberg University: its
    Organization and Development 1962
Stolee, M. J.
—The Seminary's Part in Recruiting for the Ministry 1928
Strempke, Vernon L.
—Admittance Norms and Procedures 1955
—Articulation between Colleges and Seminaries in the Selection
    of Persons for the Ministry and other Church Occupations 1961
Streng, A. C.
—The Religious Influences at Lutheran Junior Colleges in United
    States and Canada 1932
Strom, Carl W. (US Inspector of Consular Service)
—International Cultural Relations 1952
Stump, J.
—What Pre-requisites should be demanded for entrance to our
    Lutheran Theological Seminaries 1918
—Dogmatics and the Modern Theological Curriculum 1924
—The Church and the Theological Seminary 1927
Sullivan, Robert F.
—Developments in Graduate and Special Schools 1963

T

Tanner, Jacob
—The Spiritual Experience of Students in the Seminary 1935
Taylor, Charles L.
—Theology for Everyman: as the AATS Sees It 1962
—Significance of Accrediting Agencies: AATS 1962
Thye, Edward J. (U.S. Senator)
—Address at Dinner Meeting 1952
Tilberg, W. E.

R. E. Morton
President, Dana College
Blair, Nebraska
NLEC
Vice-President, 1952
President, 1953

F. C. Wiegman
President, Midland College
Fremont, Nebraska
NLEC
Secretary-Treasurer,
1942 - 1945

OFFICERS OF THE CONFERENCE

H. S. Oberly, Ph.D.
President, Roanoke College
Salem, Virginia
NLEC
Vice-President, 1961
President, 1962

L. M. Stavig
President, Augustana College
(S.D.)
NLEC
Vice-President, 1960
President, 1961

143

EXECUTIVES OF THE CHURCH BOARDS SERVE ON
NLEC COMMITTEES

Arthur Ahlschwede

Executive Secretary,
Board for Higher Education,
The Lutheran Church-
Missouri Synod

E. T. Bachmann, Ph.D
Executive Secretary,
Board of Theological Education,
Lutheran Church in America

EXECUTIVES OF THE CHURCH BOARDS SERVE ON NLEC COMMITTEES

Norman Fintel

Executive Secretary,
Board of College Education,
American Lutheran Church

F. C. Gamelin, Ph.D.

Executive Secretary,
Board of College Education
and Church Vocations,
Lutheran Church in America

CHAPTER III

Program of Services to Colleges and Seminaries

Although the service of the Conference was directed to the colleges and seminaries, often, both directly and indirectly, the service was of value to the member boards of college and theological education. This was true from the point of view that this service removed the necessity for the board's working in the same direction, or it relieved the boards from spending as much time and money for services in certain areas. Only the secretaries of boards can be fully aware of this situation. This can easily be understood for the period 1958 to 1967.

Because of the space given to the annual meetings and the subjects discussed at these meetings in Chapter II, nothing special need be said about the annual meetings in this chapter, even though they were considered a real service to the member institutions and to the cause of inter-Lutheran cooperation. In fact, for many years the program of the Conference consisted only of an annual meeting at which presidents (or their representatives) of colleges and seminaries discussed matters and problems of mutual interest and shared valuable information. This is one of the reasons which urge the continuation of this Conference as a corporate entity. A free association of seminaries and colleges, which have much in common, so far as service to the church is concerned, will always be of great benefit to those who attend and share information about developments at their schools. This judgment was repeatedly confirmed through the years in oral statements and written letters.

The proceedings and papers were not published until 1919 and then continued through 1942. Beginning in 1943 to 1959 inclusive, the papers were not published primarily on account of lack of funds. This hiatus is rather regretable as is shown by a reading of the volumes which were printed. It is true that not all papers were equally valuable for publication.

This chapter on Program of Services will include historical data and facts concerning the News Bulletin, Publicity and Promotion, Research Projects and Studies, the Placement Bureau, and the Faculty Fellowships.

A. News Bulletin

As early as 1922 the secretary of the Conference at that time, Dr. H. D. Hoover, sent a communication to the Conference (he could not be present on account of the death of his father), stating, "Your secretary feels there is room for a mimeographed monthly news bulletin about what our institutions are doing." The following year, 1923, the Conference resolved:

146

"That the Lutheran Bureau of the National Lutheran Council be requested to send out at such stated intervals as the Bureau may deem necessary, a mimeographed report of news items of the various colleges and seminaries which are members of this Association."

In 1924 the Conference voted for a special committee to "consider the problem of the publication of a periodical devoted to the interests of Lutheran Educational Institutions, and of the Lutheran teachers in Lutheran and non-Lutheran schools." The officers were constituted as this Committee and were given power to act with the proviso that they make no arrangements which would in any way involve the Conference financially. At this time it was suggested that "The Lutheran Survey" would perhaps be willing to set aside a certain number of pages in each issue for the use of the Conference.

It was not until 1932 that the Conference took a definitive step in the direction of a News Bulletin. At that time, Gould Wickey was the secretary and raised the question whether it was "possible and desirable for this Conference to issue a monthly news bulletin." He indicated that he, as executive secretary of the Board of Education of the United Lutheran Church in America, had started such a bulletin for his colleges and seminaries "and the results have been so much more beneficial than had been anticipated, that your secretary believes something of that sort might have similar value for this Conference. . . . **Such a bulletin may be a step in the direction of a greater Lutheran unified consciousness."** Accordingly, the Conference recommended a Lutheran Educational News Bulletin as valuable and desirable, and voted,

"That a working agreement with the News Bulletin of the National Lutheran Council be sought, whereby the cooperation of as many as possible of our educational institutions may be enlisted and the Bulletin be given a proportionately wide distribution. We recommend that the officers of the Association be granted power to act in the matter."

The records show that in September 1932 appeared the first issue of the News Bulletin of the National Lutheran Educational Conference, under the editorship of Gould Wickey, who was the Conference's secretary. At first, and until February 1939, it appeared as an issue of the NEWS BUREAU OF THE NATIONAL LUTHERAN COUNCIL.

In February 1935, Dr. Mary E. Markley assumed the editorship when Dr. Wickey became the Executive Secretary of the National Conference of Church-Related Colleges and also of the Council of Church Boards of Education. Dr. Markley continued as editor until 1947 when she retired from the office of secretary of the Board of Education, ULCA. Then, Dr. Wickey again assumed the editorship and has continued through 1966.

The bulletin was issued bi-monthly from 1935 to 1947. Finances caused a reduction in the issues to a quarterly basis in 1948. From 1945 to, and including 1948, the copies of the News Bulletin in the records of the Conference are incomplete. For this situation this author cannot account.

A distinctive feature of the News Bulletin during several years under the editorship of Dr. Markley was the presence of an editorial written generally by a college or seminary president, or the editorial was obtained from other sources.

According to the information available, from September 1932 to December 1966, there were 203 issues with the number of pages totaling 1466. These contents may be categorized as notes of colleges and seminaries 760 pp; studies 60 pp; books by faculty members 38 pp; special articles or editorials 142 pp; editorial notes 243 pp; and miscellaneous items 223 pp. The distribution or mailing of this Bulletin in 1958 was 3,500, which was 300% more than any previous year, but in 1966 the number reached 5,000. It was sent in bulk to faculty members of the member schools, and individually to church officials, members of boards of education and boards of directors.

The volume for 1966 contained the largest number of pages of any volume, namely 60 pp, and received perhaps the largest number of comments in the history of the Bulletin. The results of several studies were reported in brief which were quite informing and of special value to the presidents and faculty members. For example, there were 18 pages containing the names of authors and titles of their books printed during the past five years. Nothing like this had ever been published by any Lutheran agency. The study of gifts and grants to Lutheran colleges and seminaries, related to the Conference, was quite revealing. It showed that the gifts and grants for 1964-65 amounted to $31,211,189, while those for 1963-64 amounted to $21,915,563, — an increase of 42.4%. Lutheran church bodies were surprised to learn that their grants to their own colleges and seminaries were only 37.1% of the total gifts/grants which these schools received.

Since copies of the *News Bulletin* are not easily available, it is desirable to note some of the editorials and articles which elicted considerable reactions. For the sake of any who have access to a complete file of the Bulletin, the name of the author, the title of the editorial or article, and the date of the issue are given.

O. H. Pannkoke, The Next Steps in Lutheran Higher Education, Jan. 18, 1935.

A. Steimle, A Suggestion for our Colleges, (undated but included as a special late in 1936. It was read before a meeting of *Koinonia,* a Lutheran ministerial club in New York.)

C. M. Granskou, Christian Education on the Offensive, Mar. 17, 1939.

T. F. Gullixson, At What Levels Shall Men Fish for Men? Sept. 15, 1939

Evald B. Lawson, Do our Students Live by the Bread of Great Ideals? May 17, 1940

Bernhard Christensen, The Spiritual Foundation of Freedom. Sept. 20, 1940

Ruth Immel, A Call to Women. Nov. 15, 1940

T. A. Kantonen, The Pastor's Ten Commandments. Dec. 20, 1940

John A. Pettit, Forgive our Christmases. Dec. 12, 1941

Henry J. Arnold, Fighting for Survival. Sept. 25, 1942

O. F. Nolde, Toward a Better World Order. May-June 1945.

C. G. Shatzer, Called into Court, December 1945.

Gould Wickey, Ecumenicity within the Lutheran Church, December 1947.

Gould Wickey, The President Studies Higher Education. Jan.-Mar., 1948.

Erland Nelson, Predictions of a College President. Apr.-June 1949

Gould Wickey, Suggestions for Evaluating the Campus Religious Life. July-Sept. 1950.

Ernest C. Colwell, Ten Commandments for College Presidents. July-Sept. 1952.

Edgar M. Carlson, New Horizons in Lutheran Higher Education. Jan.-Mar. 1953.

W. L. Young, Implication for Christian Higher Education in the Merger of Lutheran Church Bodies. April-June 1953.

Amos J. Traver, Shall Seminaries Teach Writing? July-Dec. 1954.

W. A. Russ, Jr., Training is not Education. May-June 1958.

Gould Wickey, A Decalogue for Church-College Graduates. May-June 1958.

George Anderson, The Christian Teacher, as seen by a University Professor. May-June 1959.

Robert P. Stripling, Orientation Practices for new College Faculty Members. May-June 1961.

Gould Wickey, The Image of the College and the Admissions Office. Jan.-Feb. 1964.

J. Pelikan, The Whole Truth. Sept.-Dec. 1964.

Carl T. Rowan, Education in the Post-Modern World. Mar.-April 1966.

Naturally, through the years many comments were received about the values of the *News Bulletin*. Frequently, members of boards of directors would send in comments indicating that the contents were of value to them in fulfilling their responsibilities as members of boards of directors of colleges and seminaries. The president of a prominent money-raising firm wrote: "Let me congratulate you on the recent Issue of the *News Bulletin*. I have read every word of it with great interest and benefit. You are rendering an outstanding service in the work you are doing in this important position. . . ." The dean of a college included these sentences in a letter,

"I would like to express once again my appreciation for the bi-monthly *News Bulletin* which you edit. I depend upon your fine publication for the important news taking place in Lutheran colleges and seminaries in our nation." The president of a prominent Lutheran college wrote, "This last issue of the *News Bultin*, full of news as it is, is only one of the features of the work of the Conference which have helped to keep us informed and **to give us a feeling of solidarity as Lutheran institutions."**

Mildred E. Winston, Litt.D.

Secretary, Board of Education, ULCA, 1928-1961, and of the Board of College Education, LCA, 1961—

NLEC
Archivist, 1947-1955

Mary E. Markley, Litt.D.

Secretary, Board of Education, ULCA, 1919-1946

NLEC
Editor, News Bulletin, 1935-1947
Vice-President, 1936

Horace F. Martin, Ph.D.
President, Midland College
Fremont, Nebraska
NLEC
Secretary, 1927-1929
President, 1930—

Orville Dahl, Ed.D.
Secretary, Board of Christian Edu-
cation, Ev. Lutheran Church
Later, President,
California Lutheran College
Thousand Oaks, Cal.
NLEC
Secretary, 1952-1957

Harold L. Yochum
President, Capital University
Columbus, Ohio
NLEC
Vice-President, 1949
President, 1950

Evald B. Lawson
President, Upsala College
East Orange, N. J.
NLEC
Vice-President, 1957
President, 1958

153

James C. Kinard

President, Newberry College
Newberry, S.C.

NLEC
Vice-President, 1939, 1942-44
President, 1940, 1941

Sidney Rand

Executive Director, Board of Christian Education, ELC and ALC
and
President, St. Olaf College,
Northfield, Minn.

NLEC
Active on important committees.

B. Public Relations: Publicity and Promotion

A study of the Resolutions (noted in chapter II) and the various steps taken in the area of public relations reveal the great interest which the Conference had in this subject. However, it should be noted that the interest was not so much for itself as for its membership, — the colleges and seminaries. This is seen in 1911 when a special committee was appointed "to consider the feasibility of, and plans for, an active and general campaign throughout our Church in America in behalf of Christian education." Nothing much was accomplished in this direction until the latter part of the 1920s when it seemed possible that the various Lutheran church bodies would have simultaneous campaigns for Christian higher education. Various conditions and factors prevented the achievement of those simultaneous campaigns, which were foreseen and expressed at the informal meeting of representatives of Lutheran church bodies and educational institutions, held in Chicago on March 14, 1928, such as recent campaigns have already been staged by many institutions, the time was not opportune in some sections, some feared such simultaneous campaigns would indicate a type of unionism, some people were tired of financial campaigns, and some simply did not care to put forth the effort which all such campaigns, financial or educational, require.

In the 1940s and 1950s some success was achieved in the cooperation between boards of education in their promotion of the cause of Christian higher education. The definite results of these efforts are not in the files of the Conference, but it is known that the Conference in 1935 urged "joint publicity for our institutions of higher learning" and that the boards of education of the American Lutheran Church, of the Norwegian Lutheran Church and of the United Lutheran Church did at times issue joint publicity items and/or purchased items from one another for use in their own promotional efforts.

Christian Education Sunday was used to good effect by the Conference, when on the Sunday of the annual meeting, pastors of the city where the meeting was held were urged to invite an educator, college or seminary, of their own church body or otherwise to speak at the morning service. This plan was followed quite extensively in the 1930s and 1940s. Sometimes an evening service was held in which all congregations were invited to cooperate. Later, in the 1940s, the Council of Church Boards of Education planned Sunday evening meetings that same Sunday, which meant that all Protestant denominations cooperated in this emphasis and the Lutheran meeting was discontinued.

Promotion, in some form, was frequently on the programs of the annual meetings. The work of Dr. Emerson Reck of Colgate University, and later of Wittenberg University, was of special value for information and encouragement in this field to the schools.

In 1938 at the annual meeting slides and films of some schools were shown. In 1940 began a period when the Conference had exhibits of some sort during the annual meetings, generally near the registration desk.

At the meeting of the Lutheran World Federation in Minneapolis in 1957 an extensive exhibit of pictures and printed materials from the schools was presented. Dr. Sidney Rand, then executive secretary of the Board of Christian Education, Evangelical Lutheran Church, represented the Conference in the preparation of that exhibit. The Board contributed a sum towards the art of the exhibit, in addition to what the schools contributed.

For exhibit at the Lutheran Center in the World's Fair, the Conference gathered pictures and printed material from the schools. Also, the Conference paid the sum of $1,500 for the Melanchthon memorial column in the court of Christian Pioneers, Protestant and Orthodox Center. This column and seven others were dedicated to Lutheran pioneers at noon on Lutheran Day at the Fair, July 19, 1964. The Rev. A. O. Fuerbringer, president of Concordia Seminary, St. Louis, Mo. was president of the Conference and placed a floral piece before the Melanchthon memorial column. (This item is referred to in chapter II).

At some of the annual meetings the local newspapers generally cooperated in supplying desirable pictures and giving, sometimes, an extensive coverage of the program of the Conference.

Some of the pictures and some items of publicity and promotion are retained in a loose-leaf binder on the subject for the Archives.

The releases from the national office received attention from the Lutheran religious journals and received desirable coverage through the Religious News Service. Annually the enrollment studies elicited extensive coverage. Other studies, such as salaries, costs and building programs also seemed to merit news releases, even occasionally in the New York Times. This was especially true with the study of the building programs released in October, 1965. This study showed that more than $175,000,000 worth of buildings were in process of construction or definitely planned for Lutheran campuses in North America. The News Bureau of the National Lutheran Council gave valuable cooperation in obtaining a wider area of publicity through a three-page release.

The only pieces of promotional printed matter, put out by the Conference in recent years, were two folders, entitled, "Why You Should Support a Quality Education at Lutheran Colleges and Seminaries Now" (1960), and "More Power at Lutheran Colleges and Seminaries" (1962), each one with a ten thousand printing. These were used to interest individuals in the Martin Luther Fellowship Program to assist the colleges and seminaries in obtaining more full-time faculty members with the earned doctorate through aiding such faculty members without the earned doctorate to obtain the same. While these promotional efforts were not

156

pushed too much, they did result in attracting the interest of a number of individuals who contributed sums from $5.00 to $1,000. (This Fellowship Program is discussed at length in Section E of this Chapter.)

C. Research Projects, Studies and Surveys

From time to time in the history of the NLEC, committees or commissions were appointed and authorized to study certain problems and to report to the Conference; at other times they were appointed and allowed to report or to present what they thought to be desirable and of interest to the membership at the annual meeting. In 1922 these commissions are noted as: Commission on Survey, Commission on Lutheran Literature, and Commission on Courses in Bible and Religious Subjects.

In 1923 the Commission on Survey gave a preliminary report indicating that they would survey (1) General Relationship, Service and Aims; 2) Equipment, Endowment, and Income; and 3) Faculty, Curriculum and Student Activities. This Commission reported that such a survey

1) will furnish a definite body of information which can be used by college executives in a study of their administrative problems, and which can be used as a guide in working out their expansion programs;

2) will indicate both the strength and weakness of the Lutheran educational institutions in this country;

3) will in some measure at least determine a set of minimum standards for Lutheran educational institutions;

4) will provide for college executives who wish to use it for that purpose a definite statement of urgent needs of the institution which can be used in presenting these needs to individuals, boards and bodies throughout the Church and to the larger philanthropic agencies; and

5) will increase respect for us on part of non-Lutheran institutions.

It is quite evident that this commission had thought through its problems in that day in a very thorough manner. But there was to be no travel to and visiting of institutions. The whole work of the survey was to be carried on through questionnaires.

We have not been able to ascertain what happened to this survey. There is no report available which would indicate that the survey was completed. It is probably for this reason that the Board of Education of the United Lutheran Church in America decided to ask Columbia University (Teachers College) to make a survey of its colleges which was completed in three volumes in 1929.

In 1948 three Commissions were authorized: Commission on Theological Education, Commissions on International Student Exchange (later changed to International Cultural Cooperation), and a Commission on Research and Surveys. In 1951 another commission was appointed: Commission on Public Relations. Sometimes an individual would make an extensive report on some special study in which he had been interested. Some of these reports were incorporated in the minutes in various forms, others were inserted in the Record in typed or mimeographed form, and others were part of the Report of the Executive Secretary of Director. The results of some of these studies, during the period, 1958-1966, were sent directly to the presidents of the colleges and seminaries, especially those dealing with salaries, costs, gifts and grants with an indication of where the particular institution stood in relation to the other schools. However, the Conference was informed of the fact of the studies and sometimes given the results in summary form, which was generally considered sufficient for the Conference as a whole. Frequently, the executive director made studies which were considerd confidential and for the presidents only.

The results of these studies are not reproduced in this history. Persons interested in the studies and surveys should refer to the records of the Conference and/or to the printed proceedings. Naturally, the confidential studies were not published. Copies of some of the studies are included in the Archives in a loose-leaf binder under the caption of Studies and Surveys. A list of most of the studies is included in later pages.

The survey of Bible Teaching and Allied Subjects in Lutheran and non-Lutheran colleges and Secondary Schools in 1923, as well as the survey of Bible knowledge of college students in 1925 no doubt had some influence on effecting a more adequate study of the Bible in Lutheran colleges with quality standards and some emphasis on the spiritual.

For a few years in the 1950s the executive secretaries were considered the committee on research and studies. Regular oral reports were made to the Conference. Early in 1949, the Board of Education of the Evangelical Lutheran Church took action to the effect of inviting the Boards of Education of various Lutheran church bodies, "to participate in a joint survey and study of Southern California with a view to possibly establishing a four-year junior college in the Los Angeles Area." For more than a generation the Lutherans in California were urging their parent boards of education to consider this matter. So the executives of the boards of education of the Evangelical Lutheran Church, J. C. K. Preus, of the American Lutheran Church, William L. Young, and of the United Lutheran Church, Gould Wickey, became active in gathering information and in preparing sections of a possible report. Secretary Wickey was chairman of the Committee. In 1951 Orville Dahl became executive director of Higher Education of the Evangelical Lutheran Church and was made a member of the Study Committee on California. About 1955-56 Robert Mortvedt became a member of the Committee through his becoming the executive of the board of education of the Augustana Lutheran Church.

At the meetings of the NLEC in 1953 at Los Angeles and in 1954 at Cincinnati this committee presented some of the results of their study, and various phases of the problem were discussed. In 1954 the committee put its report in print under the title, "Lutheran Educational Possibilities in California," and had it widely distributed to the various boards of education and to all Lutheran pastors in California. The effect on the boards, and the Lutheran Church bodies in California was positive and optimistic, so that in 1958 the California Lutheran College was established on a two-year basis, but it soon had enough students for a four-year college. The NLEC contributed $200 towards a distribution of this Report among the Lutheran clergy in California.

Another significant study was authorized directly by the Conference without significant results. For many years at the annual meetings questions such as these were asked: What is the Church's responsibility in education at any and all levels? does the Lutheran Church have a philosophy of education, — of parish education and of higher education? is the philosophy of Lutheran education different from that of Christian education? should we speak of a Christian philosophy of education, or a philosophy of Christian education?

At the annual meeting in 1962, the Board (Executive Committee) appointed a special committee with authority, composed of Conrad Bergendoff, then president of Augustana College, Rock Island, Illinois; O. P. Kretzmann, president of Valparaiso University, Valparaiso, Indiana; and Sidney Rand, then executive secretary, Board of College Education, American Lutheran Church. Gould Wickey, executive director of the Conference was appointed consultant. The committee held a couple meetings during which extensive consideration was given to the problems involved. Finally, it was decided to hold a conference on "The Lutheran Church and Education", at Williams Bay, Wisconsin on May 2-4, 1963. To this conference were invited individuals of the three major Lutheran bodies, including representatives of theological seminaries, colleges, parish education, and public education both secondary and higher. The two-day conference was deemed very much worthwhile, but the depth of exploration revealed distinct difference in perspective, evaluation and terminology. After a study of the tape-recording, which was not satisfactory, the committee asked five individuals to prepare essays on assigned subjects which were presented in the proceedings of the 1964 annual meeting of the Conference and later in a brochure for extended distribution. The essayists and their subjects were: O. P. Kretzmann, "Education under the Cross at 4:00 P.M."; Conrad Bergendoff, "The Educational Implications of Christian Faith"; Allan O. Pfnister, "The Relation of Education and Vocation"; Harold Ditmanson, "Excellence in Christian Education"; and Bernhard Christensen "The Quality of the Christian School".

The chief tangible result of that Williams' Bay Conference was the production of a brochure entitled, "Some Perspectives on Christian Higher Education", published in 1964. The brochure enabled many faculty members to study and to think through aspects of a philosophy of Christian education in a more definite manner and no doubt has influenced the thinking and conclusions of some. If it has done that, the conference was not in vain.

A Chronological List of Research Projects, Studies and Surveys

This list includes only such studies as were authorized and persons were invited to prepare by the NLEC. Generally, partial reports of Committees on Studies are not noted. From 1958 to and including 1966 some of the studies especially the annual enrollment survey, are included in the annual report of the Executive Director. This officer also made quite a number of studies, which are designated by the initials GW, and the results of which were either presented to the annual meeting of the NLEC in summary form or were reported to the presidents of the institutions directly. All enrollment studies were made under the direction of Gould Wickey with the able assistance of office staff.

1920 Educational Institutions (Lutheran) with Statistics (Appended to printed proceedings)

1923 Survey of Bible Teaching and Allied Subjects in Non-Lutheran Colleges, Lutheran Colleges, and Secondary Schools by Heisey, Bostrom and Martin

1923 Survey Commission on Lutheran Colleges, — a report of progress

1925 Survey of Bible Knowledge of College Students .... J. F. Krueger

1926 Salary Schedule of College Teachers .... H. F. Martin

1930 Methods of Teaching in College .... Julius Bodensick

1933 Motives for Attending Lutheran Colleges (19 pp) ...... Erland Nelson

1934 Need for Lutheran Literature (37 pp) .... John O. Evjen

1936 Problems of Personnel Work in Lutheran Colleges
    1. Philosophy and Aims .... M. J. Neuberg
    2. Personnel Services .... C. A. Serenius
    3. Tools and Techniques .... Laurence J. Schaaf
    4. Personnel Administration .... Erland Nelson

1936 An Investigation of certain Factors affecting the Scholarship of College Students .... M. J. Neuberg

1937 Attitudes of Lutheran College Students .... Erland Nelson

1937 Church Membership of Students. See printed Proceedings, pp 98-99
    Enrollments at Seminaries. .... See printed Proceedings p. 100.

1938 Statistics of Lutheran Educational Institution ...... Mary E. Markley

1939 Enrollments

1940 Enrollments

Job Analysis of Personnel Functions in Lutheran Colleges ....
M. J. Neuberg
Freshman Orientation in Lutheran Colleges, etc. ...... Erland Nelson
1942 Enrollments
Women Students in Lutheran Colleges .... Mary E. Markley
1947 Survey of Finances at Lutheran Colleges .... E. Lindquist
1947 A Study of the Practice of Subsidizing Ministerial Students ....
E. E. Flack
1948 A Report on Displaced Persons .... Mildred E. Winston
1948 Survey of Incomes, Budgets, Building Fund Campaigns and
Procedures in Lutheran Colleges and Universities belonging to
NLEC .... Emory Lindquist
of Personnel Practices .... W. F. Zimmerman
of Admission Practices .... Herbert G. Gebert
1950 Summary of Faculty Studies and Research at Lutheran Colleges ......
Johannes Knudson
Review of Productivity of Lutheran College Faculties in past 10
years .... E. Lindquist
Non-American Nationals on Lutheran Educational Institutional
Campuses .... H. J. Arnold and Mildred Winston
A Study of the Product of the Lutheran College ....
C. M. Granskou and C. H. Becker
1951 A Study of Faculty Women in Lutheran Colleges Mildred E. Winston
1952 Occupational Survey of Alumni of Lutheran Colleges—report of
progress by Commission on Research
1953 Enrollments
1954 Enrollments
1955 Enrollments
1956 Enrollments
Exhibits of Grants to Lutheran Colleges by the Ford Foundation
G. W.
1957 Enrollments
1958 Enrollments
1960 Centuries of Service by Lutheran Colleges and Seminaries ...... G. W.
Enrollments in report of the Executive Director
1960 A Study of the Length of Service of Presidents .... G. W.
1960 A Study of Grants for Graduate Studies pertaining to Teaching in
Lutheran Colleges and Seminaries as given by Lutheran Church
Bodies (Boards of Education) and their Schools by G. W.
1961 Enrollments in report of the Executive Director
1962 Enrollments in report of the Executive Director
1962 An Exhibit of the Founding of Lutheran Colleges and Seminaries
in the United States and Canada during the developments of the
Lutheran Church in the United States and Canada .... G. W.

1963 Enrollments in the report of the Executive Director
1963 A Study of Voluntary Support in Lutheran Schools as compared to the national study noted in the Annual Report of the Council for Financial Aid to Education .... G. W.
A Study of Responsibilities and Opportunities of Lutheran Higher Education and World Understanding .... G. W.
1964 Enrollments in the report of the Executive Director
1964 A Study of Administrative Salaries at four-year Lutheran Colleges .... G. W.
A Study of Faculty Salaries at Lutheran four-year Colleges .... G. W.
A Study of Salaries: Faculty and Administrators at Lutheran Junior Colleges .... G. W.
1964 A Study of Costs at Lutheran four-year Colleges .... G. W.
1964 A Study of Gifts and Grants to Lutheran Theological Seminaries during 1963-64 .... G. W.
1965 A Study of Gifts and Grants to Lutheran Theological Seminaries during 1964-65 .... G. W.
1965 Enrollments in the report of the Executive Director
1966 Enrollments in the report of the Executive Director
1966 Enrollments in the report of the Executive Director
Seminary Enrollments, 1941-44 to 1961-64 .... G. W.
Gifts and Grants in report of Executive Director

D. Placement Bureau

Concern about obtaining an adequate number and well-trained teachers was prominent in the discussion of the members of the Conference. In 1916 President J. A. Morehead of Roanoke College moved,

"That a Committee of Three be chosen to arrange for a Central Bureau of Teachers to list teachers eligible for Lutheran college positions and submit the list to college presidents."

Evidently, not much was accomplished by this action, since in 1923 a request was made to the Lutheran Bureau of the National Lutheran Council "to open a Teachers' Bureau, in order to assist Lutheran Educational Institutions in finding capable professors and instructors when they are needed."

However, something was being done in this direction by the Board of Education, ULCA. In 1921, 1922 and 1923, Dr. F. G. Gotwald, the executive secretary, sent out mimeographed bulletins, called "Board of Education Service and Teachers' Bulletin". The 1921 bulletin had 8 pp; 1922, 17 pp; and 1923 18 pp. (Copies are in the archives of NLEC)

This work of the Board of Education, ULCA and the 1923 resolution of the Conference resulted in 1924 in the publication of a Directory of Lutheran Teachers with 58 pp; in 1925 with 72 pp; and in 1927 with 88 pp. (Copies are in the archives of the Conference) These directories were helpful, but finances apparently were not available for the continuation of such publication, for in 1931 the Conference voted, that "the publication of the Directory of Lutheran Teachers be not continued at this time." However, it was suggested that information regarding "each such prospective teacher be mimeographed on a single sheet and forwarded to our schools promptly for their information and filing. This was to be done by the secretary. Evidently, the publication of the Directory would not reach the presidents' offices in time of need.

The Board of Education, ULCA, under the leadership of Gould Wickey as its executive secretary, had established what functioned as a placement bureau and made the information available to all the institutional members of the Conference. In 1934 the Conference formally expressed its appreciation "of the work of the Teachers' Placement Bureau under the direction of Dr. Wickey."

However, the Conference continued to feel that it, as a Conference, ought to establish a Lutheran Teachers' Placement Bureau, and so voted in 1947 that such should be done "in conjunction with the Student Service Commission of the National Lutheran Council." The Conference directed its Executive Committee "to expend up to $1,000 annually for this work". The minutes and financial statements of the Conference indicate that payments were being made annually to the Board of Higher Education, ULCA for its expenditures in this service with Gould Wickey as the director of the Conference's Placement Bureau. In 1955 the expenditures amounted to $123.59.

The Board of Higher Education, ULCA took action at its December 11, 1957 meeting, which greatly encouraged the Conference to take a progressive step at its meeting in 1958. The action of that Board of Higher Education reads,

> "Whereas the Board of Higher Education, ULCA has learned of the possibility that the National Lutheran Educational Conference would establish an office in Washington for the purpose of developing an effective program for the placement of teachers in Lutheran Colleges and seminaries, and for encouraging youth in preparing, through graduate studies, for teaching positions in Lutheran colleges and seminaries, and

> "Whereas, the Board of Higher Education, ULCA for some twenty-five years has been interested in this two-fold program, and

> "Whereas, there is unusual need for teachers in Lutheran higher education,

> "Therefore, Be it Resolved, That the Board of Higher Education, ULCA encourage the National Lutheran Educational Conference in this proposed step, and promise what cooperation may be possible in the development of the program".

Since the ULCA Board of Higher Education moved its offices to New York City in February 1958, it offered most of its furniture and facilities to the Conference for its office in Washington. This included the facilities for a Placement Bureau.

In 1955 the Board of Higher Education, ULCA had obtained a full-time secretary for the Placement Bureau, Miss Gertrude Belzer, with experience in this field. Some 2,000 names of Lutheran teachers at non-Lutheran schools had been obtained through the Division of College and University Work, NLC. Some of these persons were interested in teaching at a Lutheran school, and a goodly number (56) had been so placed.

With more adequate facilities, with adequate secretarial service, and with a considerable number of names of prospective teachers and administrators for both colleges and seminaries, the Placement Bureau of the Conference was off to a good start in 1958.

The work of a Placement Bureau includes much detail and recording of such details, if the service is to be fully effective and appreciated. There is the preparation of various blanks for registry; then there is the recruiting program; and there is the receipt and duplication of the registration blanks, all of this information being placed on Keysort cards. After schools submit information about vacancies and request dossiers, there is the task of studying the cards and the information blanks for persons suited for the particular vacancy. Thereafter follows the preparation of dossiers for the vacancies,—sometimes four or five being sent for one vacancy, and each dossier may include as many as six sheets. A careful record of these details is necessary for accuracy in any report.

Some figures about the Placement Bureau from 1958 to 1966, inclusive, will be of interest:

<pre>
Registration blanks requested and mailed   1,905
Dossiers mailed with about 6 pp. each   5,597
Recruitment letters mailed biennially
    ranged from ....   1,600 to 4,103
</pre>

Because of failure to report placements, it is impossible to give an accurate figure for the number of placements. There is a record of more than 210; we believe that 300 more accurately indicates the fruit of this service. In terms of dollars, the NLEC saved the schools and/or the prospective teachers/administrators, on the basis of the cost of a commercial placement service, from $60,000 to $75,000.

This placement service was greatly appreciated by college and seminary presidents and deans, and also by those who were placed. Constantly, deans wrote to the office expressing their appreciation, generally in such terms as, "I want to express my appreciation for your cooperation in our search for suitable candidates." The director of a research agency wrote, "I was much impressed with the service you provide." A Lutheran at a

State University College, hoping to join the faculty of a Lutheran college, wrote, "I am most appreciative of the fine and efficient way in which you have handled my situation in the past. The Placement Bureau should be commended."

E. Martin Luther Faculty Fellowships

As early as 1910, in fact at the very first meeting of the Conference, there was approval of "the establishment of one or more fellowships for the training of teachers in connection with our Lutheran schools." So far as the available records are concerned, no definite steps were taken in the direction of establishing teaching fellowships until in 1957 when Dr. Conrad Bergendoff expressed at length his concern for the welfare of the Lutheran colleges at the point of their teaching personnel. With this in mind, Gould Wickey prepared a comprehensive program for the extension of the work of the Conference and included a plan for graduate fellowships. This was presented at the 1958 meeting and met with unanimous approval.

The plan called for (1) screening of applicants, whose names had been received from colleges, seminaries, and workers with students at universities; (2) financial grants relative to the needs of the applicants and the total amount of funds available; (3) a Committee on Selection which would screen the applicants and determine the amount to be allowed in each case; (4) a follow-up of those receiving grants inquiring as to the standard of their work; and (5) placement in Lutheran schools and follow-up on standard of work. This plan was carefully carried out with the exception that there was not a systematic follow-up as to standard of work after a fellow was placed. The holders of fellowships were called Martin Luther Fellows.

Although only approved at the January meeting of the Conference in 1958, the program was put into effect with the beginning of the academic year, 1958-1959. The Lutheran Brotherhood Insurance contributed $15,-000 and the Conference used $1,450 of its funds, making a total of $16,450 which was distributed to 16 applicants. For the eight academic years during which the Fellowship Program was in effect, 256 grants were made to 185 individuals, in a total amount of $363,620. The grants ranged from $300 for summer study to $2,000 for an academic year. A fellowship could be renewed for a second year. The grants averaged $1,420.

A large stimulus to the program was the grant of $50,000 from the Lilly Foundation during a two year period. Of course, the continued co-operation of the Lutheran Brotherhood Insurance in a total of $204,150 was really the backbone of its success. The Lilly grant was made on a matching basis, and as an encouragement to the boards of higher education of the Lutheran Church bodies, whose boards were members of the Conference, to give more attention to this problem for their schools and to support the program of the Conference. A portion of the dues of the member institutions and boards was used each year for the fellowship program.

Here follows an exhibit of the number of grants for each year, the total amount distributed, and the sources from which those funds were received.

Year	Number Grants	Total Granted	LBI	Lilly	NLEC
			Sources of the Funds		
1958-59	16	$16,850	$14,550		$ 2,300
1959-60	33	41,550	20,250	20,000	1,300
1960-61	43	60,150	20,700	30,000	450
1961-62	31	43,050	30,000		13,050
1962-63	36	52,200	26,000		26,200
1963-64	37	53,700	30,000		23,700
1964-65	38	61,120	26,150		34,970
1965-66	22	35,000	27,500		7,500
Totals	256	363,620	204,150	50,000	109,470

It should be noted that the amount indicated as coming from the Lutheran Brotherhood Insurance, was paid directly to the grantees, selected out of the total number approved by the LBI as part of its Faculty Fellowship Program. The Conference Committee on Selection screened all applicants and allowed the LBI to select the persons whom they would take as their own. The LBI prepared blanks for obtaining information from the applicants similar to those of the Conference.

Further, it should be pointed out that of the $109,470 indicated as coming from the Conference, some $63,700 was given to the Conference by boards of higher education, $9,599 was contributed by individuals, and the balance $36,171 came from the dues of the members.

The Grants from the various boards of education for the Faculty Fellowship Fund were as follows:

Board of Christian Higher Education, Augustana Lutheran Church $ 3,000
Board of College Education, American Lutheran Church 29,700
Board of Higher Education, United Lutheran Church 11,000
Board of College Education, Lutheran Church in America 20,000

Total 63,700

The number of applications for fellowships was generally twice and sometimes three times as many as the funds could allow. Consequently, at the 1962 annual meeting, after the Executive Director had reported on the Fellowship Program, two resolutions were made from the floor, which were approved, as follows:

"That the officers of the NLEC personally approach the Lutheran Brotherhood Life Insurance Society for the sum of $100,000 as an annual grant for the MARTIN LUTHER FELLOWSHIP

PROGRAM because of the great need of more teachers with the earned doctorate in our colleges and seminaries."

"That a formal request to the Ford Foundation and other Foundations be made by the officers of the NLEC on behalf of the Martin Luther Fellowship Program as a cooperative enterprise."

The officers were not successful in obtaining favorable action on the part of the Lutheran Brotherhood Insurance Society, the Ford Foundation, and other foundations.

The Executive Committee (Board of Directors) presented a special recommendation to the 1966 annual meeting of the Conference to discontinue this fellowship program as follows:

That, since boards of education, college and theological, of the various Lutheran bodies related to the NLEC have greatly increased their scholarship and fellowship programs, especially during the past six years, and

since national foundations and the U.S. Government have established and are establishing scholarship and fellowship programs in terms of millions of dollars, especially during the past five years, and

since it appears that there is a special need at this time for larger concentration on faculty discovery and placement,

Therefore, be it resolved, that the NLEC deems it unwise to continue its Martin Luther Fellowship Program.

This recommendation was unanimously approved, since there was some evidence that the church boards of education would be able to care for most of the needs of the colleges and seminaries in assisting faculty members to complete their graduate studies and obtain their doctorates. In spite of all that the boards are doing in this field, the NLEC received more than 60 inquiries about fellowships in 1966.

The personnel of the Committee on Selection was changed frequently during the eight years so that a total of 24 persons participated. The executive director was chairman through all the years and the presidents of the Conference participated as members. The following functioned on the Committee on Selection at some time: A. Ahlschwede, G. Arbaugh, E. T. Bachmann, C. Bergendoff, P. Dieckman, E. Fendt, N. Fintel, A. Fuerbringer, F. Gamelin, D. Heiges, O. P. Kretzmann, W. Langsam, E. Lawson, R. Mortvedt, K. Mattson, S. Oberly, S. Rand, R. Seeger, L. Stavig, M. H. Trytten, W. Wolbrecht, W. Young, J. W. Ylvisaker and G. Wickey. The Conference repeatedly expressed its appreciation to this Committee for its service. All members took their responsibility very seriously and spent much time in screening applications. Attention should be called to the fact that Dr. Raymond Seeger, National Science Foundation, and Dr. M. H. Trytten, National Academy of Science, are not members of any Lutheran faculty and served for five years, the longest of any other members, except the chairman, Gould Wickey.

As to the results of this program, at least 60 reported receiving the earned doctorate and 24 obtained masters' degrees, by the fall of 1966. The status of the 185 persons aided through the program is as follows:

Now teaching in a Lutheran School 138
Teaching in a non-Lutheran School temporarily,
    awaiting appointment in Lutheran Schools 8
Employed in a Lutheran agency 7
Pastor in a Lutheran Parish 4
Still engaged in study 22
Information incomplete, generally
    awaiting placement in Lutheran School 6

It is understood that some who are teaching or otherwise placed are continuing their studies for the completion of their doctorates.

This fellowship program has been a distinct factor in assisting the colleges and seminaries to increase the number of faculty members with the earned doctorate. During the short period of 1960 to 1966 the seminaries and the colleges related to the NLEC have greatly increased their academic excellence through the addition of more full-time faculty members with earned doctorates. In 1960 the seminaries had only 40% of their faculty members with earned doctorates; in 1966 the figure jumped to 57%. Seven of the fifteen seminaries, related to the NLEC, have more than 60% of their faculties with the earned doctorates. The senior colleges in 1960 had 28%, while in 1966 they had 39%, of their full-time faculty members with the earned doctorates. Thirteen of the thirty-one Lutheran colleges, members of the NLEC, have more than 40% of their full-time faculty members with earned doctorates. No detailed study has been made to ascertain exactly how many of the present faculty members were holders of Martin Luther Fellowships, but in spot studies of certain schools the evidence is very strong as to the importance of this fellowship program in adding earned doctorates to the faculties of Lutheran colleges and seminaries.

As a matter of historical interest, the names of the fellows together with the years when they were given fellowships and their fields of interest are listed below. In some cases the field of interest may have changed during the course of their studies from that indicated at the beginning of their studies. The Conference has in its files the titles of the doctor's theses by those who have thus far obtained their doctorates. It was thought not necessary to publish those at this time, especially since more will obtain their degrees within a few months after the publication of this history. It would be desirable in a few years, say 1970 by which time all degrees should be received, to make the titles known to the schools which are members of the Conference.

Martin Luther Faculty Fellows, 1958-1966

As an item of historical interest, it is desirable to record the names of the Martin Luther Fellows, the years when they received grants, and the field of graduate study. All these names were screened and approved by the Conference's special Committee on Selection. From the approved list, a Committee of the Lutheran Brotherhood Insurance selected certain names to whom they gave grants directly for their particular fellowship program. The total number of different fellows amounted to 185, and the total amount of all grants was $363,620. If more than two grants are indicated, it means that the grants were for summer or part-time study and that the total was not more than $4,000.

Name	Year of Grant/s	Field of Study
Anderson, Albert B.	1958-59, '59-60	Phil. of Religion
Anderson, Charles S.	1959-60, '60-61	Church History
Anderson, Dorothy M.	1959-60	Education
Anderson, Robert L.	1962-63	Ethics
Anderson, Roger W.	1961-62	Education
Andrews, Paul H.	1962-63	Theology
Bakken, Norman K.	1959-60	Biblical Studies
Baldwin, Roger	1964-65	Sociology
Bansen, Norman C.	1960-61	Literature
Barnett, Robert J., Jr.	1958-59	Classics
Bauge, Kenneth L.	1960-61, '61-62, '62-63	Economics
Baumbach, Bernard C.	1964-65, '65-66	Sociology
Beamenderfer, Jean	1961-62	Business Adm.
Beckman, Peter T.	1963-64	Theology
Bella, Igor V.	1962-63, '63-64	Dogmatics
Benson, John E.	1965-66	Phil. of Religion
Bent, Roy S., Jr.	1961-62, '62-63	Phil. of Religion
Bertram, Robert W.	1961-62	Theology
Bittrich, Louis E.	1963-64, '64-65	Literature
Bjorgan, G. Rudolph	1960-61	History
Bland, Richard M.	1964-65, '65-66	Linguistics
Bolton, Fred J.	1961-62	Theology
Boraas, Roger S.	1960-61	Old Testament
Bossart, Philip C.	1962-63	Psychology
Bost, Raymond M.	1959-60, '60-61	Church History
Brandon, Esther J.	1963-64	Guidance
Bretscher, Paul G.	1964-65	Theology
Brown, Raymond K.	1959-60	Physics

Buck, Erwin	1963-64, '64-65, '65-66	New Testament
Bunge, Wilfred F.	1964-65	New Testament
Butler, Bartlett R.	1959-60	Musicology
Carroll, Glenn E.	1964-65	Human Relations
Cartford, Gerhard M.	1959-60, '60-61	Musicology
Christiansen, C. Arthur	1959-60	Biology
Christiansen, C. Gerald	1965-66	Church History
Dahlberg, Duane A.	1964-65	Physics
Davidson, Mary E.	1961-62	Nursing
Decker, John DeWitt	1960-61	Biology
DeMott, Howard E.	1960 Summer	Biology
Dipple, Elizabeth	1959-60, '61-62	English
Diskerud, Clayton L.	1964-65	Education
Doermann, Ralph W.	1958-59	Old Testament
Eckstein, Neil T.	1964-65	English
Eggold, Henry J.	1961-62	Theology
Ehlen, Arlis J.	1961-62, '62-63	Old Testament
Ewing, Morgan R.	1965-66	History
Faris, Bernard G.	1964-65	English
Fesperman, Francis I.	1962-63, '63-64	Religion
Foss, Harold F.	1963-64	Biology
Frank, Clovis S.	1961-62	Classics
Franti, Charles E.	1959-60	Education
Frear, Graham S.	1965-66	English
Frerichs, Wendell W.	1965-66	Old Testament
Fretheim, Terence E.	1963-64, '64-65	Old Testament
Gerhardt, Ray C.	1961-62, '62-63	History
Glebe, Delton	1959-60, '60-61	Psychology
Govig, Stewart	1961, '62, '63, '64 (summers)	Philosophy
Graesser, Carl, Jr.	1961-62, '63-64	Old Testament
Gram, Harold A.	1962-63 Summer	Economics
Griffith, Mildred	1958-59	Economics
Grill, F. Russell	1959-60, '60-61	Philosophy
Gunderson, Lloyd A.	1965-66	Languages
Gusenius, Edwin M.	1959-60	Chemistry
Guss, Evelyn G.	1960-61	Classics
Halverson, Wm. H.	1960-61	Philosophy
Halvorson, John V.	1961-62	Old Testament
Hamlin, Joe R.	1964-65	Rhetoric
Hammann, Louis J. III	1963-64	Philosophy
Hansen, Leif E.	1965-66	Literature

Hanson, John R.	1963-64, '64-65	Ethics
Hatz, Russell C.	1963-64	Music Education
Heffley, Robert W.	1958-59	Old Testament
Hefner, Philip	1961-62	Theology
Heinze, Rudolph W.	1961-62, '62-63	History
Helgeson, John G.	1965-66	Theology
Helms, John	1960-61	Classics
Hemmingson, A. Robert	1960-61	Economics
Hess, Elmer B.	1965-66	Geography
Heussman, John W.	1964-65	Library Science
Hofrenning, James B.	1963-64	Religious Education
Holte, Carlyle W.	1959-60, '60-61	Theology
Hoppe, Ralph	1958-59, '59-60, '65-66	Amer. Literature
Iverson, Joseph G.	1963-64	Education
Jackisch, Frederick F.	1962-63	Music
Jennings, Wm. H.	1962-63, '64-65	Ethics
Johnson, Clair E.	1962-63, '63-64	Homiletics
Johnson, Dale A.	1962-63, '63-64	Church History
Johnson, Einar O.	1959-60	Education
Johnson, Marlowe W.	1960-61, '64-65	Music
Jordahl, Rodger S.	1961-62, 1962 Summer	Old Testament
Jensen, Robert	1959-60	Theology
Kadai, Heino O.	1963-64	Church History
Kalin, Everett R.	1964-65, '65-66	New Testament
Karatzas, George	1965-66	Economics
Keller, Walter E.	1964-65	New Testament
Kennedy, James G.	1960-61	English
King, Alvin	1962, 1963, Summers	Music
Kirsch, Paul J.	1960-61	Religion
Kissell, Gerald N.	1960-61	Phil. of Religion
Knudsen, Keith D.	1959-60, '60-61	English
Knudten, Richard D.	1961-62, '64-65	Church History
Koskenmaki, Joyce	1960-61, '61-62	Fine Arts
Kramer, Melvin L.	1962, Summer	Business Education
Kretzschmer, Blaise	1961-62	Theology
Kurzweg, Bernhard F.	1962-63	Homiletics
Lang, Reuben C.	1965-66	History
Langen, Robert B.	1959-60, '60-61	Philosophy
Laube, Richard H.	1962-63, '63-64	Business Adm.
Lee, Knute W. D.	1958-59	Religious Education
Leeseberg, Martin	1960-61	Old Testament
Levin, Arnold G.	1963-64, '64-65	New Testament

171

Lillehaug, Leland A.	1960-61	Music Education
Lindgren, Alice L.	1958-59, '59-60	Zoology
Lucas, James L.	1960-61, '63, '64	English
Lundeen, Joel W.	1959 Summer	Library Science
McCune, Mrs. Marjorie	1965-66	English Literature
McCurley, Foster R. Jr.	1963-64, '64-65	Old Testament
McKean, Joel M.	1960-61, '61-62	Mathematics
Manthei, Donald W.	1960-61, '62-63	Psychology
Marple, Dorothy J.	1962-63	Personnel Adm.
May, William R.	1965-66	Semitics
Menges, Robert J.	1960-61	Psychology
Menn, Joe K.	1960, 1961 Summers	
	1963-64, '64-65	History
Meyer, John S.	1964-65, '65-66	Statistics
Mezoff, Earl R.	1962-63	Education
Mohr, Martin	1960-61	English
Monhardt, Maurice E.	1963-64, '64-65	Music
Montgomery, John W.	1958-59, '61-62	Biblio History
Moore, Carey A., Jr.	1958-59	Semitics
Moretz, Walter J., Jr.	1962-63, '63-64	Church History
Muedeking, George H.	1960-61	Education
Naeseth, Erling	1959-60	Economics
Niedenthal, Morris J.	1963-64	Homiletics
Nissen, Eugene W.	1962-63	Classics
Nuechterlein, H. E.	1960-61	Music
Olafson, Robert B.	1962-63, '63-64	Literature
Olson, Eric H.	1960-61	Political Science
Olson, Jeannine Fahsl	1963-64	History
Osborn, Howard H.	1961-62	Entomology
Otterness, Omar G.	1962-63, '63-64	Theology
Paschke, Louise Ann	1958-59	English
Pearson, Birger A.	1962-63, '63-64	New Testament
Pederson, Arne K.	1960-61	Education
Pirner, Reuben G.	1962-63	Theology
Podoll, Darryl	1964-65	History
Prauner, Edwin E.	1960-61	Economics
Ragan, Gilbert C.	1965-66	Economics
Rast, Walter E.	1963-64	Bible
Refsell, Lloyd G.	1962-63, '63-64	Theology
Reinberger, Francis E.	1958-59, '59-60	Religion & Psychology
Reneke, James Allen	1959-60	Mathematics
Renninger, Jesse B.	1958-59, '59-60	Old Testament
Ringham, Stuart R.	1965-66	Political Science
Ritzman, Dean F.	1958-59	History

Roa, C. Durward	1963-64, '64-65	Psychology
Rulon, Russell, R.	1958-59	Physiology
Saarinen, Martin F.	1960-61	Education
Santmire, Harold P.	1961-62, '62-63, '63-64	Theology
Satrom, Merlyn E.	1961-62, '62-63	Theology
Savage, James S.	1961-62	Law
Scheifele, Theo. C.	1964-65, '66	Sociology
Schiller, Johannes A.	1963-64	Sociology
Schmidt, Warren	1959-60	Music
Schroeder, Donald P.	1959-60	German
Schutte, Thomas F.	1960-61, '61-62	Economics
Sechriest, Ralph E.	1958-59	Biology
Sigel, Charles P.	1962-63	Classics
Sponheim, Paul R.	1959-60, '60-61	Theology
Streiker, Lowell D.	1964-65	Religion
Streng, Adolph Jr.	1959-60	Rel. Psych.
Stucke, Doris G.	1964-65	Nursing (Ed. Adm.)
Stuhr, Walter M.	1964-65	Ethics
Sulouff, Nelson R.	1961-62, '62-63	Old Testament
Svendsbye, Lloyd	1959-60, '60-61	Church History
Swanson, Stanley H.	1960-61	Religion (Compar.)
Teigen, Ragnar C.	1960-61, '63-64	Old Testament
Thomas, David E.	1961-62	Social Ethics
Trone, Robert H.	1964-65	History
Wagner, Norman E.	1964-65	Old Testament
Wegner, Walter	1964-65	Hebrew Studies
Weis, James M.	1965-66	Church History
Westlund, Virgil R.	1962-63	Church History
Wilson, Howard A.	1959-60, '63-64	Religion
Winter, Herbert	1960-61	Political Science
Wolf, Herbert C	1961-62, '64-65	Theology

If these fields of study are summarized under comprehensive categories we find that the 185 Martin Luther Fellows made these selections:

Religious and Theological Education 77
Liberal Arts 45
Physical Sciences 11
Social Sciences 52

Nine of the fellows selected subjects in the field of religion, which were included in the 77, but which might as well be included under another category, especially since most of them are teaching or will teach in colleges. Some who studied theology are now teaching in colleges.

The pictures related to the Fellowship Program are the only ones available for this purpose.

General Willard Paul, president of Gettysburg College, left, joins in congratulating Robert J. Menges and Joel M. McKean as Gould Wickey, executive director, NLEC, presents the Martin Luther Fellowship awards on Founder's Day, April 8, 1960. Mr. Menges (second from left) studied psychology at the University of Chicago and Mr. McKean studied mathematics at the University of Pittsburg.

William H. Halverson, left, assistant professor of philosophy and religion at Augsburg College, Minneapolis, receives a Martin Luther Fellowship Award, as a Lutheran Brotherhood Faculty Fellowship from
Ruben Egeberg, standing, district representative of the Lutheran Brotherhood Insurance, while President Bernhard Christensen observes. Mr.
Halverson studied at Princeton University 1960-61. Dr. Christensen was
president of the NLEC during 1945.

President Martin J. Neeb (left), Concordia Senior College, Fort Wayne, Ind., congratulates Professor Herbert Luechterlein on his selection for a Martin Luther Fellowship Award to study in Germany during 1961 in the field of Kantorei at the time of the Reformation. Dr. Neeb was president of the NLEC during 1960.

President J. W. Ylivisaker (left) Luther College, completing his year as president of NLEC, observes while Gould Wickey, executive director of NLEC presents a Martin Luther Fellowship check to Albert B. Anderson (center) to study at Harvard University in the field of philosophy. This was the 50th anniversary (1960) of NLEC with the meeting held in Boston, Mass.

President O. P. Kretzmann, Valparaiso University, Indiana, looks on while Gould Wickey, executive director, NLEC, presents a Martin Luther Fellowship Award to Professor Richard Laube to study business administration at the University of Nebraska during 1962-1963.

President A. O. Fuerbringer, Concordia Seminary, St. Louis, congratulates Professor Walter Wegner upon his receiving a Martin Luther Fellowship for study in Hebrew at the University of Wisconsin, 1964-1965. Dr. Fuerbringer was president, NLEC in 1964.

CONCLUSION

The Past as Prolog to the Future

When is the Past Prolog?

In a paper read before the annual meeting of the NLEC in 1965, discussing "the Church and the Government of the Educational Institutions." Norman Fintel, executive secretary of the Board of College Education, American Lutheran Church, said,

> "This is a new generation today in Lutheran higher education, which knows not Kretzmann, Pannkoke, Bergendoff, Granskou, Boe or Wickey. We do not know much about the momentous days of the 1920s and '30s when much of the really pivotal work in Lutheran higher education was taking shape. The new generation needs a similar experience. It has a vast advantage over that important earlier contingent because it can build on their work. But time is short; 1970 is almost here; 1980, 1990 2,000 are around the corner. What will we have accomplished by the Twenty-First Century?"

That statement was somewhat shocking to some of those who heard it, since five of the six names mentioned were living, and one or two of them were actually at that meeting. A hasty hearing of those words naturally caused some to think, and, perhaps, to say, "Well, that's too bad." But it seems the writer of those words was really thinking not so much about the persons mentioned as about "the momentous days of the 1920s and 1930s when much of the really pivotal work in Lutheran higher education was taking shape." When Mr. Fintel went on to say, "The new generation needs a similar experience," he indirectly answered the question placed at the beginning of this chapter, "When is the Past Prolog?" Certainly, the past is not prolog to the future merely because of sequence of years. The past is really prolog only when the present is fully cognizant of the basic principles upon which the present is built, and, of course, of the principles which the past failed to utilize in building the present.

While, logically, this history precludes a conclusion bearing on the future, but rather should include some summary of the evaluation of the past, nevertheless the very purpose of this Conference as an ongoing corporate organization does call for some reference to the possible direction which Lutheran higher education should take in the future. The basic purpose of the Conference in 1967 is the same as was implicit in the first meeting in 1910. It is more fully and explicitly stated in the revised Constitution considered at the 1967 annual meeting and reads as follows (see also the first chapter):

180

"The purpose of this Conference shall be to consider problems in higher education, especially as related to Lutheran higher education, to share information, to suggest strategy, and to encourage and to assist the member institutions in their programs of Lutheran higher education as they serve the Lutheran Church and develop a Christian leadership for Church and Country."

So in harmony with the spirit and vision of the past and the stated purpose of the present Constitution of this Conference, the author concludes this history with some suggestions which may help to make the constructive Lutheran educators of the past effective in future Lutheran higher education through the present corps of able administrators, the boards of education, and the educational institutions.

What the Future Needs

1. *An Ecumenical Point of View*

From the very beginning in 1910 the point of view of this Conference was ecumenical. As Dr. Gotwald wrote and is quoted in the first chapter, "The policy of this Conference has not been exclusive but inclusive." All educators were interested in the problems of other institutions and had a desire to help solve those problems. Christian education is part of the work of the Lutheran Church, and every Lutheran group, even just to be loyal Lutherans, dare not neglect the education of children and adults.

It is necessary that there be a medium of communication between the Lutheran colleges and seminaries related to the Lutheran Council in Canada and those schools related to the Lutheran Council in the United States of America. This Conference, carefully named, Lutheran Educational Conference of North America, is such a bridge.

In addition, this Conference is the only Lutheran educational organization which can include the colleges and seminaries of Lutheran groups not related to the Lutheran groups included in the above named councils. This is most significant, for we believe that conversations and dialogues must be continually held between and with the colleges and seminaries of all and any Lutheran groups.

Not only is this Conference interested in Lutheran colleges and seminaries, but it has through the years been interested in Lutherans related to non-Lutheran educational institutions and organizations. There were many years when this interest was not manifested as it should have been. But for the past ten and perhaps fifteen years, through the Placement Service, this interest has been manifested and great appreciation has been expressed. The very fact that more than a hundred such perhaps have been individual members, paying a $5.00 fee, annually during recent years shows the possibilities in this direction. This individual membership was obtained without any special effort.

Further, this Conference should manifest more interest in what Lutheran pastors at non-Lutheran colleges and universities are doing. Their work is part of an educational and evangelical program which is vital to the life of the Lutheran Church wherever it may be. Although officials of the various student service groups have appeared on the program of the Conference, as groups and the individual pastors of these groups should be contacted and cultivated constantly. With their experiences at non-Lutheran schools, they have a contribution to make to the total program of Lutheran higher education.

Still, further, this author has experienced the interest of Lutheran lay men and women not related to any Lutheran educational institution. In fact sizeable sums of money came to the Conference for its fellowship program from the laity during the past ten years. Throughout both countries there are business men, lawyers, doctors, persons in government service and other fields of activity, who could be interested in membership in this Conference. They may not be able to attend annual meetings but they would be willing to make payments of an individual membership fee and to receive the printed documents of the Conference.

2. *Continued and Increased Cooperation*

It was the mutual sharing of information and suggestions which made the first meeting in 1910 so significant that it was decided to develop a permanent organization. Again, Dr. F. G. Gotwald informs us of the situation at the first meeting, when he writes in the introduction to the 1919 volume (actually the first ever published), "The meeting was so valuable and successful that the informal conference was regularly organized and perpetuated."

Representatives of all Lutheran educational institutions, from Canada and the United States, whatever the Lutheran group to which they may be related, seated together considering their problems, encouraging one another, devising a common strategy for special and unusual situations, and many other conditions would undoubtedly be of great benefit to most of the schools, — even the larger schools. It will be a tragic day if and when the Lutheran schools in the United States isolate themselves from the Lutheran schools in Canada, and vice versa. It will be a tragic day when the colleges in either country try to isolate themselves from one another, likewise with the seminaries. It will be a tragic day when the seminaries of the Lutheran Church isolate themselves from the Lutheran colleges which are a source of a large percentage of the seminary enrollments, and prefer rather to be related to non-Lutheran universities. Both types of institutions perform both an educational and a church function.

All this means that the programs of the Conference must be of interest to the representatives of both the colleges of liberal arts and the theological seminaries. It has been done in the past; it can be done in the future.

With the growth in the institutional membership and the possible growth in the membership of individual Lutheran educators, it would seem advisable to develop Sections, such as a Section on Liberal Arts Colleges, a Section on Theological Seminaries, a Section on Junior Colleges, and a Section on Boards of Directors of institutions. As early as 1911, it was suggested that members of Boards of Directors be present. In recent years the responsibilities of Boards of Directors have come to the front more and more. These sections could have parallel programs and then come together for all-inclusive sessions. This would probably require more than a total of three sessions; perhaps five as was held for many years.

The question has been raised on several occasions and by various persons, whether the Conference of Lutheran College Faculties should be a responsibility of this Conference. At least, many are convinced that this Conference should be attended by more faculty members, of both colleges and seminaries. It is generally by them that the more pointed and searching questions are asked in discussion periods.

Such sections would be thinking of and studying both the present day problems facing Lutheran schools and the steps towards a long range comprehensive program of Lutheran higher education.

Here's a challenge for the greatest minds in Lutheranism to exercise depth thinking, consecrated patience and robust courage. The insight and even farsights of the fathers are not hitching-posts, but rather sign posts. Lutheran education must be concerned with the whole student, with the whole church, and with the present and the future. This is a task requiring the attention and cooperation of the various levels of Lutheran education as well as the different groups engaged in Lutheran education.

3. Promotion of Lutheran Unity

Since 1915 Lutheran educators have been most prominent in developing Lutheran unity as well as Lutheran union. In 1929 it was moved,

> "to continue with the discussion of the Promotion of Unity
> among the Synods of the Church, in view of the fact that the
> NLEC has been making every effort to secure better acquaintance
> and better cooperation among general bodies of Lutheranism
> and stands in a position to foster such relations."

A special committee should study the areas of the unity which now exists and then ascertain and explain the steps or factors upon which Lutheran unity in the future depends. As a free association of Lutheran educators without allegiance to any one group, this Conference can render this service without embarrassment to the officials of the organized Lutheran groups.

4. *Commitment to Christian higher education.*

If there be no such philosophy as a philosophy of Christian higher education; if church-related colleges attempt an educational program which is in no wise different from that offered by state or secular institutions; if there be no difference in the system of values and the moral principles presented in the class-rooms and manifested by the administrative officers; if church colleges are interested only in conforming to the conditions and situations which they find in the world rather than being themselves transformed "by the *renewing* of their minds," if church colleges are going secular more and more,—then the churches should give up their educational institutions and devote their time and money to some form of Christian service. But the Lutheran college and seminary must not adapt themselves basicly to a world which itself needs changing. Faith must not be reduced to minimal terms so that there is no faith in the highest and greatest.

That was a strong plea for distinctive Christian colleges which Dr. Robert L. Mortvedt presented in his presidential address at the 1967 annual meeting. He called for

"institutions which will strive to operate with a deep sense of commitment with respect to the formidable task of offering an excellent education *qua education* within a consciously and deliberately stated intention to encourage the search for truth within an openly declared conviction that the deepest and truest learning can be conducted within the framework of the Gospel of Jesus Christ. . . . the truest freedom that can be known is the freedom possessed by the scholar who has committed his life to Jesus Christ."

If this Conference has such a commitment, then the spirit and vision of the Lutheran educators of the first quarter of this 20th century will be carried aloft and forward into the 21st century. Then this Conference can guide our seminaries and colleges with material and method which will effect a difference in the lives of students, the life of the churches, and the outlook of our nations.

If the future needs an ecumenical point of view, continued and increased cooperation, promotion of Lutheran unity, and commitment to Christian higher education, then this Conference needs some program of service which will be an important factor in assisting Lutheran colleges and seminaries in achieving these goals.

5. *A Program of Services*

Although history looks to the past, it has a message for the present and the future. The history of this Conference suggests questions which need to be considered and answered by the present membership of the Conference.

Will an annual meeting alone fulfill the functions of this Conference? Must not a bridge between the Lutheran schools in Canada and the United States, and between the schools related to the Lutheran groups in the Lutheran Council in Canada and the Lutheran Council in the United States of America and the Lutheran schools not related to these Lutheran groups render some service which the existing divisions of educational service in the two Councils do not and will not render? An affirmative answer has become the conviction of the author as he has studied the history of the Conference for a year and has been a member of the Conference for 45 years.

As the past reviews itself and surveys the present and previews the future, it appears that at least the following program of services should be rendered *without any transgression on the assigned responsibilities of existing national Lutheran educational agencies. There should be no duplication of services.*

a. *A Medium of Communication.* There is information about basic developments in the seminaries and colleges which ought to be conveyed promptly to all the schools in the two countries. As early as 1958 a prominent college professor inquired whether it would be advisable to have a Journal of Lutheran Higher Education which would serve the interests of all the seminaries, colleges, and the student and faculty service at non-Lutheran schools. It would seem reasonable that this Conference could speak helpfully to non-Lutheran educational agencies in both countries on certain questions and under certain conditions.

b. *An Agency of Research and Study.* There are studies which could be made which would be of value to all Lutheran schools, the data for which might not be available to an agency related to certain ecclesiastical bodies. This Conference, as a free association, will have a status of confidence and objective judgment not applicable to agencies related to church bodies. This has been the definite experience of this author in the past while dealing with governmental agencies, with Catholics and Protestant colleges and seminaries.

c. *A Consulting Agency.* The very confidence which this Conference elicits makes it possible for the Conference to be a consulting agency. With an executive knowledgeable in both college and theological education, who understands and keeps informed as to their problems, who has insight as well as farsight, he can become a Lutheran educational confidant. Often presidents and other administrators of schools, as well as members of boards of directors and faculty members, wish to confer with some one not directly related to a Lutheran school and not to a Lutheran church board of education. To obtain such a person with the desirable qualifications, including sufficient experience, is no easy task, but such persons do exist and their abilities should be utilized.

The Past may be Prolog to the Future through the Present.

185